DIRECTING FILM

DIRECTING
FILM

THE DIRECTOR'S ART FROM
SCRIPT TO CUTTING ROOM

KEN RUSSELL

BRASSEY'S · INC · WASHINGTON · D.C.

Printed and bound in Spain by Bookprint, S.L. Barcelona

Volume © B T Batsford 2001

First published in 2001

Brassey's, Inc.
22841 Quicksilver Drive
Dulles, Virginia 20166

Title page image:
Ken Russell with Marilyn Monroe priestess in *Tommy*.

CONTENTS

CHAPTER I

THE PITCH

Everyone who has ever tried to get a film made is a con artist. OK, so sue me! Alright, I'll amend that: everyone who has tried to set up a movie is a liar and a cheat, or at best, a big fat fibber. And that's kosher because everyone in the industry knows that and not only makes allowances, but actually condones it. The one exception is me – in my early days, or to be honest, on my very first day. The date was January 3, 1959, with three amateur movies behind me, three children under three and at the ripe old age of 33, I was pitching for my very life – a chance to become the greatest director the world has ever known or remain a mediocre photo journalist who was the laughing stock of Fleet Street.

The editor of the photo magazine I freelanced for, had sent me to Spain to get some material on *Alexander the Great,* starring Richard Burton, which was shooting out of Madrid. He'd also arranged a free trip on SwissAir, providing I took a few publicity stills for them on the way out, with permission to shoot anywhere on the plane. For reasons now forgotten, I flew from Paris Orly at the crack of dawn. Where to start? I loaded my camera and looked around. And there it was – a paparazzi's dream come true.

Now what would that be today . . . Princess Di as an angel flown down from heaven to give him an exclusive? Or perhaps Charles caught in flagrante in the back of a Land Rover with Camilla Parker Bowles. Yes, it was that big. Well, I'm no paparazzi anyway, but it was a very big opportunity to become one, or even start a trend, for I don't think the breed even existed back in 1954. Yes, I had a scoop, an exclusive – there wasn't another photographer around for 39,000 feet.

OK, OK, I'm coming to it. The hottest scoop in the world at that minute was sitting in Row D, seats 1 and 2 – the window and the aisle. They had just secretly married and were on the first day of their secret, secret honeymoon, to a secret, secret destination nobody in the whole, wide world knew about except me. News had got out that very morning that they had just got hitched in Paris and then vanished. It was the hottest story in town, every town – it was the romance of the decade, the love story on everyone's lips, a fairy tale come true . . . wait for it – the marriage of Audrey Hepburn to Mel Ferrar!

Ancient history now, but years ago an earth-shattering event. Trembling and full of trepidation I raised the camera to my eye and focused . . . on the ecstatic lovers with stars in their eyes. I had never seen a happier couple until they caught sight of me. The stars clouded over, I was about to invade their private world and turn their summer into bleak midwinter. I lowered my camera and without as much as glancing in their direction, shamefully returned to my seat.

We arrived in Madrid and I had barely stepped into the glare of the Spanish sun, where there was still not a photographer in sight, before I heard my name being called on the PA system. It was a phone call – the editor. He was beside himself with delight.

'Get the film to the pilot. He's doing a quick turn around and flying straight back to Heathrow. We'll have it in tomorrow's first edition – world exclusive.' My reply was a verbal suicide note to my career in photojournalism.

Everything now hinged on my interview at the BBC Television Studios at Lime Grove with Huw Wheldon, who in the late 1950s was the editor of the world's first regular TV arts magazine, *Monitor*. Now was my big chance to make a fresh start with a career I'd always set my heart on ever since the age of nine, when I opened my one and only Christmas present to find a toy projector and a film of *Felix the Cat*.

Monitor had only been running a year. John Schlesinger, the resident documentary filmmaker, was about to leave to make his first feature film. A replacement was needed and Wheldon, who had seen one of my amateur movies and liked it, had granted me an interview. If I could pitch an idea for his programme that appealed to him, I'd be home and dry. His first quip, 'Bit long in the tooth to start a career in film, eh?', hadn't exactly put me at my ease, neither had his hawk-like appearance with beetling brows, beak of a nose and thrusting jaw. 'You've seen our programme, I presume, and know our style, so what do you propose?' he said.

> " . . .age of nine, when I opened my one and only Christmas present to find a toy projector and a film of *Felix the Cat*. "

(Overleaf) Still from 'Elgar', the BBC drama documentary that started the great Elgar revival. The still shows Elgar riding the Malvern Hills as a boy.

'A film on Albert Schweitzer playing Bach to lepers in the jungle,' I stammered.

And of all the pitches I have delivered since, and there have been many, none have been more certain of rejection. The hawk glowering at me from behind his massive desk metamorphosed into a thundercloud about to strike me a fatal bolt of lightning. But a split second before it could do so, I started talking – fast.

'Of course, what I'd like to do most of all is make a film on the poet laureate, John Betjeman, reading his London poems in situ.' The storms clouds lifted.

Visions of a film unit flying to darkest Africa, hiring native bearers, trekking through impenetrable jungle to film a doctor with a heavy German accent, playing boring old Bach to an audience who didn't even have the means to applaud, was not then, in 1959, the stuff to win friends and influence viewing figures. And I suspect the same would hold good for today. Just imagine the budget! Whereas dear old John Betjeman was as cuddly as a teddy bear, spoke perfect English – though not too posh – and could be filmed outside his very own door in Smithfield meat market. No air transport, no native bearers and no big budget.

'If you can shoot it in three days, with a crew of three, for 300, you're on,' said the Man of Power, now looking as pleased as punch. Seems three's my lucky number. And as things transpired, I continued to pitch ideas to Huw Wheldon at *Monitor* for many years to come with consummate success. In fact, I can only remember him rejecting one idea in twenty over the next five years. During that time, the boot was often on the other foot – as feature film producers started pitching at me.

Such a one was Harry Saltzman; producer of the Bond films, *The Battle of Britain,* and the Harry Palmer trilogy. He wanted me to make the third and last Harry Palmer. Not because of my succession of acclaimed drama documentary films, such as 'Elgar', 'Prokofiev', 'Bartok' and 'Debussy' – none of which he'd seen. But because Mike Caine, who played Palmer, had seen them and convinced him that my imaginative style of filmmaking would bring a fresh look to the series.

Harry Saltzman, no longer with us, alas, was a grey ball of cosmic energy. Grey suit, grey hair and round as a . . . well, er, ball.

'I understand you make art films,' he said at our first meeting. 'I like art, my house is full of it. And I'd like to make an art film with you. Anything special you have in mind?'

'Well I've always wanted to make a film on Nijinsky,' I said.

'Not a bad idea,' he said, 'there hasn't been a film with a race horse as the star since *National Velvet* – could be a big money-spinner.'

'Sorry, Mr Saltzman,' I said, 'I didn't mean the Derby winner, I meant the dancer.'

> **'A film on Albert Schweitzer playing Bach to lepers in the jungle,' I stammered.**

'No film on a dancer ever made money,' he snapped back.

'Then how about Tchaikovsky?' I ventured.

'Tchaikovsky's fine,' he said. 'In the meantime, if you wanna break into features you've gotta start off with a sure thing. *The Ipcress File* and *Funeral in Berlin* were big box office bonanzas and *Billion Dollar Brain*'s gonna be the biggest yet. Get that one under your belt, get yourself a name and then we'll talk Tchaikovsky. Your first feature film is all important.'

'But I've already made a feature film, Mr Saltzman,' I foolishly ventured, '*French Dressing*.'

'That doesn't count,' he retorted, 'they tell me it was shot in black and white.'

And so he talked me into it.

Some time later when I reminded him of his promise he was deeply offended that I'd had the effrontery to bring it up. *Billion Dollar Brain* was not the box office hit Harry had hoped for, so he was less than happy when I reminded him of his promise to let me make a film on Tchaikovsky, but as it happened he had a marvellous 'out'. 'Too late,' he said triumphantly. 'Dimitri Tiomkin's gonna make one for the Soviets and he's already writing the music.'

Russell showing 'Elgar', the drama documentary, to the makers of the *Monitor* TV programme, (left to right) Alan Tyrer (film editor), Ken Russell, Huw Wheldon, Peter Cantor (assistant editor).

Huw Wheldon and Peter Cantor
of the *Monitor* TV programme
with Ken Russell, working on the
'Debussy' drama documentary at
BBC Elstree studios.

(Right) Russell and Huw
Wheldon discussing 'Isadora
Duncan' at the Elstree studios.

Well, I did get to make that film on Tchaikovsky, but Harry didn't produce it, United Artists did. They had financed and distributed *Billion Dollar Brain*, and talked me into directing *Women in Love*. Although the Harry Palmer movie had only made a respectable financial return, the D.H. Lawrence movie went through the roof, so understandably, they were going to look with a friendly eye on any other movie I might propose. But at the mention of the word Tchaikovsky, their faces fell. 'What's it about?' they asked mournfully.

'It's about a homosexual who falls in love with a nymphomaniac,' I said. Without another word they gave me the money. It was the most successful pitch of my life.

Of course, luck has a lot to do with it as does belief in guardian angels and tooth fairies, and, believe it or not, even the gentlemen of the press. Or gentleman to be more precise, because the favours I have received from

them as a body can be counted on the fingers of one foot. And as is often the case, the gentleman's headline was untrue:

'Twiggy to star in Ken Russell's *The Boy Friend*.' And for once the journalist hadn't lied – I had.

Not to say I hadn't dreamed that headline often enough. Twiggy was an icon of the sixties, along with the Beatles and a bevy of present day old age pensioners of the same ilk. She was the most photographed fashion model of the decade and certainly the most popular – cockney accent 'n all. Twiggy was everywhere and wherever there was Twiggy there was Justin de Villeneuve, playing Professor Higgins to her Eliza Doolittle. Or perhaps Svengali to her Trilby would be closer to the truth. To the world he was her best friend and manager. They were a great couple and completely inseparable, speeding between fashion shoots in a posh Porsche by day and living in Arabian Night's splendour by night – encouraging me to sample a little of both.

Another thing we shared was a passion for Sandy Wilson's pastiche musical 'The Boy Friend', which paid homage to the bright young things of the roaring twenties with their doo-wack-a-doo high-stepping lifestyle, which at the time was enjoying something of a revival. Twiggy and I were both huge fans of the show and were discussing it over a glass of champagne at the Ritz one day, when we both became conscious of a lurking journalist wishing he had an ear trumpet. The occasion was the launch of a new Justin de Villeneuve superstar, in the form of a highbrow opera singer about to graduate to a career of lowbrow pop. But the nosey guttersnipe (members of the gutter press never cease sniping at me) was more interested in what we were saying than the operatic pop coming over the PA system.

'Thinking of putting Twiggy in one of your films, Ken,' he said without ceremony.'

"E already 'as,' chirped Twiggy, 'me and Justin woz shootin' down at Pinewood only larst week workin' on *The Devils*.'

The guttersnipe was gobsmacked. 'Not with all those naked nuns?' he said, sensing he had missed the scoop of the century.

'Yeah,' said Twiggy, 'we woz a couple of King Louis' courtiers in the 'Rape of Christ' scene in the cathedral. I was dressed as a boy and Justin woz in eight-inch 'igh 'eels with cupid bow lips and a blonde wig.'

Deflated, the guttersnipe sank down to join us on the settee as he hid his disappointment over the loss of a golden photo-scoop. But true to type, soon bounced back again. 'Didn't I hear you mention 'The Boy Friend'?'

'My next project,' I lied, '. . . and guess who's starring in it?'

'Not . . .?' said the guttersnipe, first gawping at Twiggy, who modestly dropped her head, then looking back to me for confirmation. I merely smiled, but that was enough to send him scuttling off to make his call.

'Cor, you 'aint 'arf gawn an' dunnit now, Ken,' said Twiggy.

Twenty-four hours later I was on the carpet in the office of the President of M.G.M. England, as he brandished the newspaper with the afore-mentioned headline.

'Are you responsible for this?' he asked grimly.

'Well yes, and no,' I said truthfully. What was coming next? A demand for me to make a humiliating public denial or what? Much to my delight it was the, 'or what?'.

'Do you think you can pull it off?' he said. 'We've owned the property for years and never knew how to handle it?'

I improvised my pitch on the spot. 'It's a great little stage show, but as it stands it would never transfer to the big screen and we have to think big . . . like Busby Berkeley who made all those big blockbuster movies in the 30s . . . make it a sort of homage to M.G.M.'s *Gold Diggers of 1933*, *Broadway Melody* and *42nd Street*.'

'What's the storyline?' said the President.

'Well,' I said, my mind racing and mindful of the *42nd Street* plot. 'Er, well, there's this little theatrical company touring in the stix. And there's a kid in the show; she's only the A.S.M., but she's a real talent and all she needs is a good break . . .'

'Twiggy?' said the President.

'Yes, Twiggy!'

'Can she dance?'

'By the time I've finished with her she'll be another Ginger Rogers.'

'And who's your Astaire?'

'Tommy Tune, great Broadway talent, all 6' 6' of him.'

'And how does Twiggy get her break?'

'She gets it . . . er, when the star of the show breaks her leg.'

'And who plays the star; you'll need a real name or it won't work.'

My mind raced; the recent Minister of Transport came to mind . . . 'Er, Glenda Jackson.'

'We couldn't afford her.'

'For me, she'll do it for love.'

The President's mind raced. 'Go on,' he said, only half convinced.

'And, of course, Twiggy's the hit of the show.'

'Is that it?'

'No, that's only half of it.'

'Tell me the other half. Where do the big Busby Berkeley production numbers come in?'

'In the mind of this Hollywood director who comes to see the show. He's thinking of turning it into a lavish Panavision movie.'

'They didn't have Panavision in those days.'

'They didn't have stereophonic sound either, but we'll have both. Anyway,

(Overleaf) Vladek Sheybal as the Hollywood director de Thrill on the lookout for talent in *The Boy Friend*.

he imagines how he'd stage the numbers and that's when we dissolve from
the small stage to the super-spectacular.'

'How about the human interest?'

'Well, apart from the usual sub-plots, De Thrill, the Producer, wants to take
Twiggy to Hollywood to star in the movie.'

'That's what you'd expect.'

'But she won't go. She gives up stardom in Hollywood because she's fallen
in love with a boy in the show and wants to stay with him in England.'

'That's all.'

'Er no, De Thrill and his long lost son are reunited.'

'His son?'

'The Tommy Tune character.'

'How does he recognize this son?'

'By the double bunny hop and the Delaware drag.'

'By the double bunny hop and the Delaware drag?'

'That's a dance step his Dad taught him when he was a kid.'

'How'd they get separated?'

'In the 1917 Revolution – they got separated in St. Petersburg when they
were touring Russia . . .'

And so it went on, with me making it up as I went along. And believe it or
not, they gave me the money to make the movie. And I'd guessed right;
Glenda Jackson did do it for love – and a canteen of silver-plated cutlery.

By and large you've got to give the moneymen something to hang their
hopes on. Once I guaranteed some investors that I could make Oscar
Wilde's *Salome* for under a million dollars. Think that's a lot of money?
Think of *Titanic* and think again.

Selling the idea of Bram Stoker's last story, 'The Lair of the White Worm',
was a doddle – he wrote *Dracula* in case you have forgotten.

A vampire film inspired by the master of the genre, with snake fangs
instead of bat teeth just has to be worth a gamble, especially when a semi-
naked Amanda Donohoe is doing the biting and sucking, and dishy
Catherine Oxenberg is sacrificed in Marks & Spencer's underwear to a
giant virgin-eating phallus.

Then there's the ploy of financing a potential new hit on the back of an
old hit.

D.H. Lawrence's *Women in Love* made money, so *The Rainbow* (which was
written first) – which not only featured the same characters and the same
Oscar-winning star, Glenda Jackson, not to mention the same Oscar-
nominated director – was an absolute cert to repeat the same boffo box
office pickings. And so it might have, if the company financing it hadn't
gone bust and withdrew all advertising on the film's first week of release.

And what if there's a film you simply have to make and no one's
interested but you. Should you, maybe, put your own money where your

Sammi Davis, Glenda Jackson and Christopher Gable with members of the Russell family during the making of *The Rainbow*.

mouth is and finance it out of your own piggy bank? Ask anyone in the industry and you'll get the same answer – 'Not on your nelly!' But thinking I'd be the exception that proved the rule, I double-mortgaged my London mansion to finance my film on the Vorticist sculptor Gaudier-Brzeska. It was called *Savage Messiah* and closed after five days in the West End. I'm now living in a small cottage in the provinces. The fact that the film is a masterpiece is ample compensation.

Riding on the success of *Tommy*, I was able to set up *Lisztomania,* by touting it as a film on a classical composer who was the Elton John of his day. No, I couldn't deliver Elton, but I could get Roger Daltrey, who starred in the title role of *Tommy,* and we all know how many millions that movie made. The fact that the treatment of the subject matter was symbolically and intellectually above the heads of the Daltrey fans was unfortunate, for the film was pure magic.

Pitching scripts in some respects is like a game of cricket. If the pitch is uneven, you could find yourself on a sticky wicket being clean bowled for a duck. And down in the cellar I've got a trunkload of mouldering scripts to prove it. Appropriately enough, one of them was 'Dracula', which I pitched here, there and everywhere at the most inappropriate time – the week three Dracula-inspired movies were released simultaneously.

I had a similar experience recently in trying to pitch 'How the West was Lost' at a time when three Westerns in a row had spelt 'tombstone' at the box office. Timing is all. For years I've been trying to get a script on the Oz composer Percy Grainger off the ground with no joy whatsoever. Then *Shine* hits the screen and suddenly everyone realises nutty musicians are big box office, especially if they come from down under. But before you could say, 'Up jumped a Swagman', some Oz promoters have jumped on the bandwagon, gone straight into production and pipped me at the post . . . which means another trip to the cellar to lay to rest yet another cherished dream cadaver. The fact that my unmade masterpiece can be run in the cinema of the mind whenever I want is some consolation, but not much.

Sometimes these buried hopes can be resurrected and, with the help of a Frankenstinian touch here and there, take on a fresh life of their own. Such was the case with another way-out composer, Alexander Scriabin, who was a man after my own heart – a true mystic who many saw as a total charlatan. The titles of his heady symphonic poems written at the turn of the century convey the altered states he hoped to induce in the minds of his audience – 'The Divine Poem' and 'The Poem of Ecstasy' being just two of them.

His music was all-embracing and, in fact, he planned to expire orgasmicly in the arms of a ravishing woman, atop a mountain of cushions in the Himalayas, while thousands of naked dancers, singers and an orchestra to match, including bells suspended from clouds of scent, would bring his masterpiece to a climax of such magnitude that the world as we know it would end in an incandescent sexual frisson with all humanity exiting the Universe on a high to end all highs.

Well, even Steven Spielberg, who can get away with pitching the most unlikely subjects, might have a problem floating that one off the ground – not to mention the hundred million dollar budget he would need to shoot it. Small wonder that unbankable little me should have a similar problem.

'Not to worry,' said a BBC producer to whom I happened to be spinning my tale of woe one day at the Beeb – where I'd just been reading excerpts from my autobiography, *A British Picture*, for a 'Book at Bedtime'. I listened avidly as he stated the obvious – which nevertheless hit me like a revelation.

'Turn it into a radio play,' he suggested, 'where half a dozen actors and the biggest sound effects library in the world can give you all these goodies and more for next to nothing.'

And he was right, as I found out after he got me a contract to adapt my screenplay for radio. There was no compromise except for the fee, which

> ❝ Pitching scripts in some respects is like a game of cricket. If the pitch is uneven, you could find yourself on a sticky wicket being clean bowled for a duck. ❞

(Overleaf) 'What the hell do I do next'. Russell on the set of 'Diary of a Nobody' shot for the BBC at Elstree Studios.

was well short of the three noughts I would have got for making the movie. Still, money isn't everything.

The other example of the Frankenstinian syndrome came about as a result of the constant rejection of a religious subject I was high on. The pitch was nice and pithy and usually went pretty well: 'It's the New Testament as Science Fiction.' . . . and that was it! And it was usually enough to raise the Studios' interest – until they read the script, that is. Too costly, too controversial, too blasphemous, were just some of the comments. But my favourite came from the head of one of the major studios:

'Not linear enough,' he said.

'From birth in the manger to death on the cross – not linear enough?' I mumbled disbelievingly as I was shown to the door. I even interested a big Italian movie mogul in the project for a while, until he was advised by the Vatican that involvement might jeopardize his entry into heaven despite his many past contributions to the Papal box office.

That was 15 years ago and the pages of the original, sole remaining script have grown dog-eared and yellow with age. But thankfully they proved all I needed to turn a slim screenplay into a fat novel, which, I kid you not, I sent off to my publisher yesterday. And who knows, if the book is a hit, one of the majors might snap up the screen rights and my little *joie d'esprit* could end up as a George Lucas blockbuster, with Brad Pitt as Jesus and music by Oscar-winner, John Williams – such is the magic of our mad, mad, mad motion picture industry.

CHAPTER II

TREATMENT TO SCREENPLAY

You can get away with indifferent photography, you can get away with unimaginative casting, pedestrian editing and uninspired music, but what you can't get away with in the process of movie-making is a bad script.

I learned the hard way on my very first feature film which had spectacular photography, a talented cast, slick editing, tuneful music, and a screenplay that sadly lacked the zest of its title – *French Dressing*.

The original idea hatched in the mind of Ken Harper, producer of the hit musical *Summer Holiday*, starring Cliff Richard and the Shadows. The music and lyrics were by the song-writing team Myers and Cass, who had been responsible for some successful intimate Revues in London's post-war West End. Here's a typical example of their style:

CURTAIN UP ON A NUN STANDING ON ONE SIDE OF THE STAGE AND A MONK ON THE OTHER. THEY SING IN UNISON:

> **"** You can get away with indifferent photography, you can get away with unimaginative casting, pedestrian editing and uninspired music, but what you can't get away with in the process of movie-making is a bad script. **"**

Marisa Mell and Brian Pringle – like 'oil and vinegar' in *French Dressing*.

'If you were the only girl in the world and I was the only boy, nothing . . .' BLACKOUT, CURTAIN.

That's it – much laughter and tremendous applause. It's funnier (just) if you know the old music hall song which was top of the bill in the year of King George VI's coronation. Yes, these boys were really with it back in the good old days of 1948.

Anyway, Ken Harper, confident they could repeat the success of *Summer Holiday*, hired them to turn his brainchild into a box-office giant. The story was simple and featured a typically English out-of-season holiday resort on the Thames Estuary. Determined to fill the empty beaches with happy holidaymakers, a deckchair attendant and a reporter on the local rag decide that if they could inaugurate a film festival starring Brigitte Bardot as Guest of Honour (and coax her into opening a nudist beach at the same time), their troubles would be over.

That's it, and lets face it, worse concepts have certainly been committed to celluloid. Jacques Tati, for instance, might well have made something of it. Come to think of it, *Monsieur Hulot's Holiday* could have been the inspiration behind that maggot in Ken Harper's brain slowly gnawing its way to the dandruff.

'Soak up the atmosphere,' said Harper when sending us off to Herne Bay, the most dismal resort in the South of England, 'and don't come back until you've written a hit.'

We were back in London the following day. Soaking up the atmosphere took no time at all. While walking on the pebbly beach at low tide, shortly after our arrival, we passed under the pier just as the loo was being flushed. While standing in our underwear in a cheap B & B, looking out at the second longest pier in Britain and waiting for our clothes to dry, we decided we'd soaked up enough atmosphere to last a lifetime and set ourselves the task of coming up with a complete storyline before the last train to London that day.

Disappointed at our early return to town, Harper was somewhat mollified at the thought of all the money he had saved on our per diems and, since he seemed pleased with our storyline, agreed to the script being written in London where everyone lived.

Next day we had another script conference - my last.

'We need to show at the start what a dead sort of town it is,' said Myers.

'Then what about the reporter getting excited over a hot news story like, er, like a funeral,' I ventured. 'The hearse – horse-drawn of course – and all the black limos of the mourners crawling along the front would be a great image, especially in black and white Cinemascope . . .?'

Myers seemed tickled by the prospect until he registered the glower of disapproval on the face of Cass, and then he, too, clammed up.

'Save your arty ideas for your *Monitor* programme on Sunday nights at the BBC, Kenneth. You're not working for a coterie of eggheads now, this is entertainment for the masses.' And the masses stayed away in droves when the film hit the West End seven months later and ricocheted into the provinces to die.

Yes, the film was a disaster. One of many from Anglo British, who also made another seaside flop starring Tony Hancock. Sheer suicide – no wonder they went bust.

Frankly, I think Myers and Cass were out of their depth: teenagers taking a holiday to Greece on a London bus accompanied by a load of catchy tunes was one thing; a social satire quite another. I smelt disaster the minute the script was delivered: the characters were cardboard cutouts and comic situations were few and far between. We'd have been better employed at Herne Bay bringing back a bunch of saucy postcards and plagiarizing them. In the event I managed to convince Harper to get another writer – a Polish intellectual engaged in writing a novel and a friend of mine. In retrospect, he should have stuck to the novel. The fact that he was a foreigner who had never been to an English seaside resort probably didn't help much either.

The mayor and corporation pose with a visiting international film star for a publicity still in *French Dressing* (centre Brian Pringle and Marisa Mell with Roy Kinnear, as press officer, far right).

The script was never right and never really ready and as the first day of principal photography drew ever closer, so the re-writes became even more frenetic. We should have put back the start date, but contracts had been signed and locations sewn up.

'We can burn the midnight oil even while we're shooting,' said Harper, 'we'll lick it into shape yet, and we can also involve the actors. Roy Kinnear and James Booth are great ad libbers. They work for Joan Littlewood's company; they improvise all the time.'

Well we actually did a lot more work on the script, which helped a bit, though we didn't involve the actors much, but more of that later.

All in all, it was a painful initiation but I learned my lesson and whenever possible only shoot scripts that I have either written myself or been heavily involved with. The exceptions were a couple of fairly recent Hollywood screenplays that I knew were far from perfect and in the best of all possible worlds should never have gone into production. But, as we all know, the film world is full of hustlers driven mainly by the almighty dollar.

French Dressing had three writers – a comparatively modest team by Hollywood standards. Comedies generally have a pretty full complement, with a veritable army of gag writers, as do disaster movies full of cliffhangers, where it's catastrophe by committee. But with more straightforward subjects I am not convinced of safety in numbers, especially in movies where the producer seems to have dragged his wife and family in on the act.

James Booth as the slap-happy deck-chair attendant in *French Dressing.*

Generally speaking, I think the fewer the better. After all, Dickens, D.H. Lawrence, Solzhenitsyn and Shakespeare managed their masterpieces without a co-writer or two. Actually I'm not so sure about Shakespeare but we'll let that pass. But looking back on my own films, I find that when the script was the work of one man, it invariably scored over those that were joint efforts – the fewer re-writes, the better. But with most writing contracts stipulating the delivery of one original script, one re-write, a revision and a polish, no producer worth his salt would feel he was getting his pound of paper unless he forced the writer to go

> 66 I find that when the script was the work of one man, it invariably scored over those that were joint efforts – the fewer re-writes, the better. 99

(Overleaf) Russell waits to make his entrance as an extra on *Mahler*.

through all those stages, no matter how perfect his first draft. This often results in the last version not being as fresh as the first.

But stop, we're jumping ahead – where exactly do we start and how? In my experience there seem to be three main categories:

1) Development of an original idea
2) An existing original script
3) The adaptation of a novel, or existing work of art

French Dressing was an original idea, as were my biographical films, *The Music Lovers* (Tchaikovsky), *Mahler, Lisztomania* and *Valentino*. Two of those I wrote myself, and two were by other writers with whom I worked closely. But in every case I was extremely familiar with the subject matter, having absorbed my subjects' lives and art for many years before committing them to celluloid. In the case of the two composers I took as a starting point their music, which by their own account was partly autobiographical.

For instance, Tchaikovsky said of his Sixth Symphony, the 'Pathétique', 'my entire life is encompassed in this music'. There were also clues in many of his other works. His Manfred Symphony, inspired by Byron's poem concerning the poet's obsession with his sister, perfectly matched the composer's feelings for his own sister, Natasha. While the symphonic poem, 'Francesca Da Rimini', with the doomed lovers consumed with guilt contemplating the abyss, perfectly expressed his anguish at being a homosexual in a hostile environment.

As for Mahler, we know that the second subject of his Sixth Symphony was a musical portrait of his wife, which tells us more in a few bars than a lifetime's research could ever reveal – not only about the woman, but also Mahler himself. That glorious theme is elevated, ravishing, passionate. In the brutal martial music that follows, we experience his jealousy over Alma's many admirers and their threat to his marriage. For as a child, Mahler lived next door to a barracks and ever after associated bugle calls and military band music with the domestic violence to which he was a frequent and highly distressed witness. And so you gradually put the pieces of this symphonic jigsaw together to end up with a colourful portrait, in which the man's life is seen through the mirror of his music.

However, this technique did not work with *Valentino*, because all his performances give a totally erroneous impression of the real man. Yes, he was a great lover, alright – but not of the ladies. So here one is thrown back on biographical material and a good deal of conjecture, which can only result in an approximation of the true man. But who cares as long as it's boffo box-office? Well, I do for one. And how I wince when I see the

> **" And how I wince when I see the words – 'Based on a True Story' – flash on the screen, because you can bet your bottom dollar it's going to be harrowing, horrible and banal. "**

words – 'Based on a True Story' – flash on the screen, because you can bet your bottom dollar it's going to be harrowing, horrible and banal. And so you are blackmailed into enduring the most awful claptrap on the grounds that the subject matter is WORTHY! Frequently they're about saints, disabled people or repentant rapists.

Our second category is the original (unsolicited) script. Most jobbing directors probably find at least one of these on their doorstep along with the junk mail, regularly once a week. Invariably they are accompanied by a letter designed to boost your ego to the skies, saying that you are the author's favourite director and that no one could do justice to their screenplay as well as you. And from the nature of the yellowing paper and the dog-eared pages, you can generally estimate how high or how low you come in their assessment of perfection. You glance at the title and if it appeals you might possibly start it over your breakfast cereal. If you are still reading it over your toast, it probably has some merit. And if you take it into the loo and finish it in one sitting, then you are definitely hooked. This has never happened to me personally. Long before then, I have usually stuck it back in the stamped addressed envelope provided, or in the absence of that consideration, dropped it in the waste bin where it belongs.

However, there was one notable exception. Some years ago while visiting my agent in Hollywood to talk about my curious career, I was given a few scripts by agency writers to while away the time on my 12-hour flight back to England. The first couple didn't survive the five-page test. One of my rules is that if there are more than five directorial instructions in the first five pages then the writer is trying to do my job. I mean things like: 'We zoom into close-up on eyeball,' or, 'We track girl along platform into lover's arms.' You'd be surprised just how common and off-putting that is.

But the third script was different. For one thing I was intrigued by the title *Crimes of Passion* and I was completely knocked out by the dialogue. I was totally involved. Didn't watch the in-flight movie, didn't buy my duty frees and hardly touched my food – BA had stopped serving caviar, anyway. The idea of a heroine who was a refined businesswoman by day and a foul-mouthed hooker by night was an intriguing one. I glanced at the title page – original screenplay by Barry Sandler. I'd heard of him – he'd written the first script on a closet gay (the name of which escapes me) ever to be produced by a major studio. He was a professional Hollywood writer and well respected.

I wondered if a treatment existed but doubted it. The fact that it came from his agency pointed to it being written out of compulsion, on spec. It probably came straight from his brain to the printed page, whereas the closet queen saga most likely started life in

> 66 The idea of a heroine who was a refined business-woman by day and a foul-mouthed hooker by night was an intriguing one. 99

Kathleen Turner as a $25-a-trick hooker waits for her next client in *Crimes of Passion*.

treatment form because as a jobbing writer he simply couldn't afford to spend months on a commercial script – especially a controversial subject that could easily get the thumbs down. No, he would have written the treatment first and got their comments on that. But a treatment for such a biting satire on the American way of death as *Crimes of Passion*, would have been turned down by every studio in town. And without the inclusion of the raunchy dialogue, no treatment could ever have done justice to

Sandler's black, black comedy. Anyway, the moment I stepped off the plane I was on the phone to my agent.

'I have to make this movie,' I said. And make it I did – but more of that later. Apart from changing the identity of the mad killer from a film buff to a Baptist minister, nothing in the script was changed. But such perfection is rare.

Oh, and before we leave this 'happy ever after' story, you may like to hear what I actually said to my agent in Hollywood and what he actually said to me.

I said: 'Why don't you get me more work?'

He said: 'Because you are not an MOR director and that's what Hollywood wants, so I can't put your name forward until they've all been rejected.'

I said: 'And how many of these MOR directors do you represent?'

He said: 'Seventy-two.'

I said: 'Goodbye.'

On looking down a list of my feature films, it appears that the majority are adaptations from existing material, mostly in the form of literary works, with a couple of musicals thrown in for good measure. The great advantage here is that the moneymen know more or less what they are getting for their investment from the start. Of course, there's many a slip 'twixt cup and lip, and the acquisition of a bestseller does not necessarily guarantee a bonanza

Russell and Jennie Linden look for inspiration in *Women in Love*.

Choosing a set up on *Women in Love*.

at the box office. Neither does the adaptation of a literary classic (the territory I am most familiar with), *Women in Love* being the prime example.

When United Artists offered me the existing script, I read it and turned it down. Until then, I'd never read a word by our most controversial novelist, and on the strength of that screenplay decided I'd made the right decision. I told my agent to contact United Artists and tell them, 'thanks, but no thanks'. Seeing 10% of my fee disappearing from his bank balance, he urged me to read the original novel before making a final decision. Against my better judgement I did so.

Two days later I was on the phone begging him to finalise my directing deal – fast! I was shattered. It was a revelation not only in its subject matter

– the literary exploration of a previously uncharted sexual jungle– but also in terms of Lawrence's cinematic style, which was virtually absent from the original script. Fortunately I was able to convince UA of this and get their blessing to restore Lawrence to the screenplay, where he was largely conspicuous by his absence. I take no credit for the re-write, all I did was to point out vast chunks of incident and dialogue that had been largely sacrificed for the writer's (he was American) own invention. I could hardly blame him – it's a Hollywood tradition to downgrade literary masterpieces so that they are comprehensible to audiences that are virtually illiterate.

Anyway, with Lawrence restored we had a hit on our hands. Even so we failed to do the novel full justice. To condense 600 pages into 120 minutes is just not possible. Something has to go, because a six-hour movie is just not on – apart from financial considerations, there is also the B.F. factor to consider: Buttock Fatigue. It's a well-known scientific fact that the human body is not designed to remain static in a sitting posture for more than two hours at a stretch. After that, we start to fidget and consequently find it more difficult to concentrate – which, all too soon, leads to boredom. As it is, most films are far too long. Take *Titanic* for instance. It would be much better at half the length, but at $120,000,000, or whatever, you can't blame the distributors for saying, forget the quality, feel the depth.

In adapting Lawrence's previous novel, *The Rainbow*, which featured the same characters, I had a much easier task, because three generations are involved here, and in choosing the last one, which led directly into *Women in Love*, I had a much better chance. Two hundred pages are easier to turn into a two-hour movie than six hundred. Whether the esteemed author would have been satisfied with my best efforts to bring two of his masterpieces to the screen, I cannot say.

They were both set in the days of the silent screen, before the fledgling art form had taken wing and learned to squawk. And whereas the best of true cinema shouldn't be a slave to dialogue (we've got radio for that), without it, in a Lawrence movie of the 1920s, you'd simply be left with lots of shots of the moon, galloping horses, stampeding cattle, naked men wrestling, and nude women singing in the rain. Actually, that could be quite exciting, but imagine the sub-titles we'd have had to endure – they would have dragged on for minutes on end. And wouldn't all that philosophising have been just an incey-wincey bit over the audiences' heads?

Anyway, Lawrence wasn't around to interfere when I made my tributes to his genius – his devoted wife Frieda had mixed his ashes with a ton of concrete and allowed it to harden, like her heart, in the backyard of their Italian villa – so I guess he wasn't too bothered. *Pace*, D.H., *pace*.

However, one living author whose novel I turned into a movie (*Altered States*) was deeply bothered, even though he'd written the screenplay himself, or perhaps I should say, because he'd written the screenplay

himself. How he cosseted that script, fussing over it like Mrs Sam Goldwyn over a pan of her precious chicken soup (on the menu at MGM for decades). It was sacrosanct!

He always carried a copy under each arm, like Moses with the tablets of the Ten Commandments. His name was Paddy Chayevsky and he was an Oscar winner several times over. Yes, Paddy was the word and the word was Paddy. He was the God of the Holy Wood scriptwriters, Lord of all he surveyed. And modest with it – a multi-millionaire living on tea and turkey sandwiches and expecting all us underlings to do the same, which became a mite monotonous after three months' hard labour. In the end the peasants revolted and feasted on steaks and St Émilion – but that's another story!

Yes, every word, every comma of a Chayevsky script had to be transferred *in toto* to the screen, and long after we'd fought it out and Paddy had been exiled to New York, I still had to call him long distance from the studio floor (where the shooting had to be put on hold) to ask permission to correct even the smallest typographical error. It was a bloodbath! Some say it brought about his untimely death a year later.

My experience with novelist Len Deighton, whose spy thriller, *Billion Dollar Brain*, was scripted by the brilliant John McGrath, was poles apart. Len didn't interfere at all, just took us both out to lunch (after he had seen the finished film) and said, 'Thanks boys, you did a great job'. What a contrast to Paddy!

(Left) Waiting for the sun in the Lake District while on location for *The Rainbow*.

(Above) Dr Joseph (William Hurt) and fellow scientists at work in *Altered States*.

So much for novels. What about plays? Well, what about them? What's the essential difference? After all, they do have quite a lot in common. You buy your ticket, sit in the dark and stare straight ahead of you trying to look over, or to the side of the back of someone's head in the hope of being entertained. True, one experience costs more and lasts longer than the other. But in that case you usually have a couple of intervals in which to vent your views, whereas with the former you have to wait until the end credits – unless you don't mind being shushed by a neighbour.

Of course, one form is dead and one is living. Both can be spectacular and magical, but the cinema has one big advantage over its rival – unless of course, you are able to sit in the front row of the stalls with a powerful pair of binoculars (which is how I always attend performances in the theatre). No, where the cinema wins hands down is with that truly amazing device: the close-up – such a bonus when adapting a play to the screen. Here, your printed play is your treatment. And unlike a novel, it can be read by a prospective backer in an hour or so. No descriptions of detailed action for page after page, no deep character analysis or philosophical claptrap here. All that has to be contained in the dialogue of the protagonists – a gift to a medium where time is of the essence.

> 66 Where the cinema wins hands down is with that truly amazing device: the close-up – such a bonus when adapting a play to the screen. 99

But there are snags – plays are, by their nature, claustrophobic, whereas cinema made its mark by bringing the big outdoors indoors and showing it to us on a big white sheet, with music. And that's what first hooks us – from our first visit to the Saturday matinée as kids, to the midnight screenings of our second childhood.

Although plays work well on radio (where the listener has to provide his own visuals), on the screen they present more of a problem. Because heaven forbid they should look stagey, which is just about the worst thing you can say about a MOVIE. Another concern frequently voiced when screen adaptations are under discussion, is, 'How are we going to open it up?', as if it were a can of worms or something. God forbid an audience should be locked in a room with a bunch of actors for a couple of hours!

Well, I reckon if you really do want to do justice to a great play, the best way you can 'open it up' to box office success is not by showing your characters going for walks or taking taxis, but to get the greatest stars in the world to head your cast. Two examples spring to mind – *Who's Afraid of Virginia Woolf*, starring the Burtons, and *A Streetcar Named Desire*, with Marlon Brando and Vivien Leigh. With riveting performances by the likes of these you don't need to show exteriors for an occasional breath of fresh air, because the performances themselves simply blow you away. Having adapted a couple of plays to the screen, I speak from experience.

The Devils, starring Vanessa Redgrave and Oliver Reed, was adapted from a brilliant play of the same name by John Whiting, which dealt with

religious persecution in the dark days of Louis XV. And while my co-stars were brilliant performers, it would be foolish to claim they enjoyed the international status of Liz and Richard.

But fortunately I had another ace up my sleeve, for my producer had also purchased the rights to a mind-blowing account of those fantastic events by Aldous Huxley, which enabled me to not only 'open them out', but turn them inside out and stand them on their head. As you may remember if you have ever read *Doors of Perception*, Huxley was no stranger to the drug experience himself, and his documentary novel *The Devils of Loudun*, is just about the trippiest version of a historical event it has ever been my good fortune to happen upon. It was also largely responsible for the original look of the film.

My film of Oscar Wilde's *Salome's Last Dance*, had the advantage of starry Glenda Jackson, but couldn't have been more stagy – deliberately! Unable, for budgetary reasons, to create the hedonistic court of horrid Kind Herod, I decided to make a virtue of necessity by presenting the play (which was banned during Wilde's lifetime) in a brothel he frequented on a regular basis, where it was to be staged as a surprise birthday present to the author by his friend Arthur Taylor, who ran the establishment.

Russell directing Michelle Phillips on the set of *Valentino*.

(Overleaf) Imogen Millais-Scott as Salome tempts Herod (Shalford Johns) with a banana.

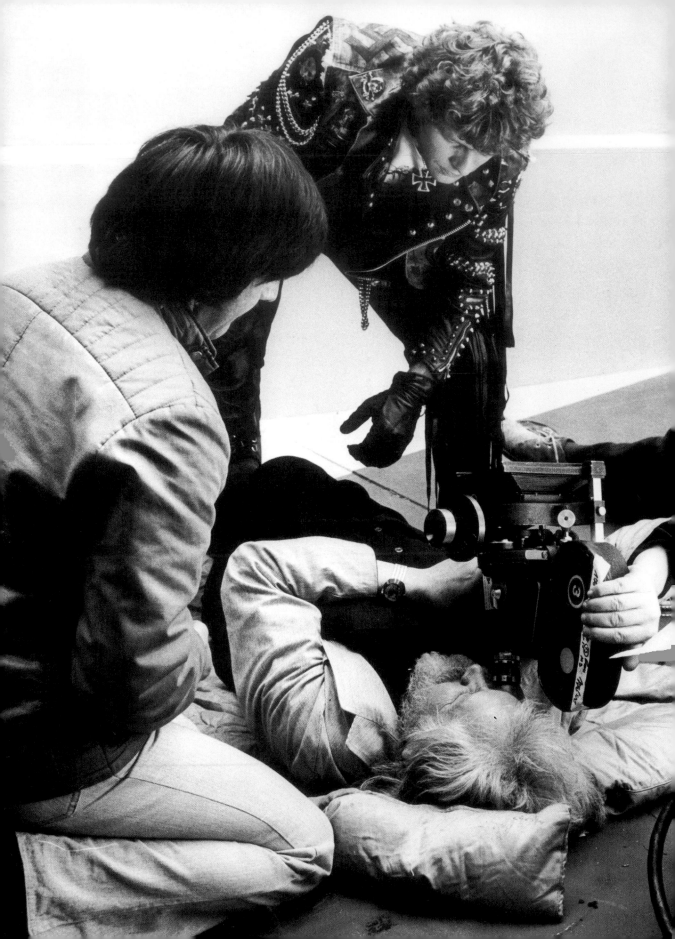

The fact that the cast included customers and courtesans alike added spice to the show. Vibrant colour both in performance and photography was instrumental in 'opening out' the play in what was an essentially claustrophobic situation. But the confines of the large drawing room in which the action took place, worked for me in encapsulating the enclosed environment of Wilde's decadent world. And this, coupled with the contrapuntal story of betrayal and Wilde's arrest on the premises, added yet another dimension to the procession of prostitutes, sado-masochists, strippers and horny midgets with which the production was littered.

As I said before, treatments take many forms, and all the potential backers of *Tommy*, for instance, had to go on was a double album of Pete Townshend's rock opera, along with the enclosed lyrics. But that was sufficient to get them hooked on the story of the deaf, dumb and blind kid who found enlightenment through pinball. That and the mega hit, 'Pinball Wizard', did the trick. Fine, except that the fifteen numbers that made up the score were all disconnected and had to be linked together to make a coherent story with a beginning, a middle and an end.

The biggest problem was the beginning: 'Captain Walker never came home; his unborn child will never know him.' See what I mean? The first thing you want to know, must surely be – who was Captain Walker and why did he never come home? So with Townshend's approval, I gave the ephemeral Captain Walker an occupation and a history – as a bomber pilot in the RAF during World War II. And to give him further substance, I showed his courtship with Tommy's Mum in the mountains, which play an important part in Tommy's spiritual journey.

The answer as to why Captain Walker never came home, is that he was shot down while on a bombing mission over Germany. And that was the start of the fascinating job of fitting together the pieces of this extraordinary musical jigsaw. So having started off with fifteen unrelated pieces, I fashioned the remaining shapes from new material so that they would all help make up a complete and comprehensible portrait of Pete Townshend's flawed Rock Messiah. And all this from a treatment contained between the cardboard covers of a double record album.

But truth to tell, I think the treatment that made most sense to the people who mattered – the moneymen – was to be found between the covers of the cashbook detailing record sales.

I was going to end it there but I can't let you go before mentioning the strangest birth of a screenplay I've ever come across. It was conceived in the back of a London taxi with the cabby himself acting as midwife. This particular bloke plied his trade in and around the Kings Cross area, which, apart from a couple of busy railway stations, is also home to hundreds of busy tarts.

Russell shooting a close-up of wicked cousin Kevin (Paul Nicholas) in *Tommy*.

Teresa Russell
plying her trade in *Whore*.

Well, everyone talks to a cabby and after a year or two, our budding writer, for that was his secret ambition, had enough material for a play in which countless unacknowledged authors had a hand. The result was a stark picture of the dangers and degradations women suffer at the hands of men. It was dynamite. Eventually I turned this shocking play into a shocking film called *Whore*.

CHAPTER III

CASTING

Casting – I tremble at the very mention of the word. It's like Russian Roulette, walking the plank in shark-infested waters, running over a bed of red hot coals, jumping into a snake pit . . . I could go on but I guess you've got the message by now. But in case you haven't, I will exercise a little of that quality eulogized by British critics, namely self-restraint and simply say – if you walk knowingly across a minefield, expect your bollocks to be blown off. So now you know why I speak in a high soprano.

Joke over, this is serious stuff. But where to start? Well, why not my very first film. It was an amateur effort called *Amelia and the Angel* and featured a 10-year-old girl who disobeys her teacher after the final rehearsal of the school nativity play, by sneaking home her angel wings to show Mum. But little brother gets his hands on them and that's that. So can Amelia find another pair in time for curtain up on tomorrow's first night? Her divine quest through some of the weirder highways and byways of London then follows, and ends, thanks to prayer and persistence, in triumph. Yes, I had just been converted to Catholicism.

Casting should have been easy. I lived in London's Notting Hill Gate at the time and was surrounded by a variety of schools – none of which, to my surprise, yielded up anyone special. The film was set to have music and commentary but no dialogue, so our heroine had to have more than a touch of charisma, as she was on the screen for most of the 25 minutes of the movie. I prayed – and the answer came from

> **"** Casting – I tremble at the very mention of the word. It's like Russian Roulette, walking the plank in shark-infested waters, running over a bed of red hot coals, jumping into a snake pit… **"**

the direction of the Argentine Embassy in the exotic shape of the Ambassador's 10-year-old daughter who was glamorous beyond her years and a bit of a tomboy to boot. All the accolades the film ever won were mostly down to her – she virtually launched my career. But there was a price to pay and she named it on the second day of shooting.

'Can we do the fast turns again?' she said as I picked her up from the Embassy in my old Morris 8 on the way to our location. She was referring to the Mews-ridden warren at the back of Kensington High Street, which we'd driven through at breakneck speed the day before, as we were a little behind schedule and needed to make up time. But I had no intention of making a habit of it.

'We're not going that way today,' I said and drove off in the opposite direction to the new location. She didn't exactly sulk during the shooting but the spark that had ignited her performance on day one was missing, and no amount of 'directing' could rekindle the fire in those Latin American eyes.

You guessed it – next day and every day for the remainder of the shoot, the fast turns always came first. And as the experience became more familiar, so I was instructed to take the fast turns at an ever-increasing rate of knots. Actually I rather came to enjoy the challenge myself and it was a small price to pay for a perfect performance. There is usually a price to pay, one way or another.

In feature films you can very rarely go with an unknown – for the simple reason that delivering a star name is generally conditional to getting the green light. To the moneymen, it's a form of insurance. One can never tell if a film is going to be a hit with the public or not, but if the star has a good track record at the box office then the project might be worth a gamble.

And, of course, there are stars of varying magnitude to suit varying budgets: giant supernovas for blockbusters, and rising stars and waning stars for lesser-budget films. Recently I was involved with one of the latter – a made-for-TV movie for Showtime, called *Dogboys*. It was a prison drama and featured a bent warden and an honest con. It was postponed twice in the space of eighteen months due to casting problems. From time to time I received video showreels from the States of prospective candidates for these two starring roles. Most of the players were unknown to me although they were apparently big names on America TV. Some were good, some were not so good. Some I passed on, some I picked. There must have been a dozen or so who could have handled the roles and given creditable performances. But they all passed on us; either because the part or the pay did not appeal.

I began to think the film would never happen, but the powers that be believed in the project and pressed on . . . and eventually their patience began to look as if it might pay off. Two bankable actors showed interest (in part because I was involved) but both had problems with the characters they had to portray, considering them both underwritten and one-dimensional. The script had gone through several drafts and may

have got somewhat diluted in the process; I can't say, having never had sight of the original.

Bryan Brown, the man the company wanted to play the baddie, wanted to know for starters why his character idolised vicious German Shepherds (I am referring to dogs here not gents in Tyrolean hats and lederhosen); and secondly, why he delighted in shooting cons with a high-powered sporting rifle. I guess he had a right to know, because he does an awful lot of both in the script. Frankly, I hadn't the faintest idea and neither, it seems, did anyone else on the project.

Bryan told me on the phone from Sydney that he had never played a baddie before and the chance to break the mould was an attractive one but he had to know where the psychotic behaviour of the nutcase was coming from. In fact he wanted to know the character's back story, so that he had something positive to work on and provide his motivation. Who can blame him? As the script stood at the time, he was just an evil, no-good bastard and that was that. The only clue that there might be more to the man than came off the page, was the fact that he listened to classical music on his Walkman while hunting down escaped cons.

Now as every filmgoer knows, if a character plays classical music in movieland, he is inherently evil and beyond redemption: characters like the wicked Captain Nemo in *20,000 Leagues Under the Sea*, playing Bach on the organ, and the insane Laird Cregar in *Hangover Square*, playing Bernard Herrmann's manic piano concerto as the house burns down. So I supposed the baddies' love of Bach was just a cinematic cliché, a sort of last straw at an attempt at characterisation. Nevertheless I grasped at it and after many attempts, came up with something that satisfied Mr Brown down under and secured from him a committed and compelling performance. I hesitate to include it here as after all the buildup, it might appear anticlimactic; but, on the other hand, I don't want to be accused of telling you a shaggy dog story either, so here goes.

Captain Brown was a prison warder in Australia, good at his job and kindly. And as compensation for being a widower, he had an eighteen-year-old daughter to dote on. She was a brilliant musician on the threshold of a solo career, having just graduated with honours from the Sydney Academy of Music. Her favoured instrument was the organ and she specialised in Bach. But her brilliant career was brought to a tragic end when she was raped and murdered by an escaped convict who also slew her pet Alsatian, which died protecting her. There it is in a nutshell, or rather, a videocassette of news clips that comes to light during our story.

Dean Cain also wanted a back story – they are all the rage these days. He was also keen to change his image – from that of a TV Superman. He was easier to satisfy than Bryan Brown and I conjured his back story out

> **"** As every filmgoer knows, if a character plays classical music in movieland, he is inherently evil and beyond redemption. **"**

of the air during a four-way telephone conversation between Dean, his agent, the TV company vice-president and myself. All we knew about our strong arm hero from the script was that he was jailed for aggravated assault after a rough-house in a local bar, during which he injured an off-duty cop.

'He was an ex-serviceman; a light heavyweight champion in the Marine Corps,' I stammered, ad libbing like mad. Believe it or not, that was enough. I was prepared to waffle on but Dean took the bait, hook, line and sinker. Apparently he was a keen athlete and very handy with the gloves, and now that he had a motivation for some fancy fisticuffs, was as happy as a . . . well, he was very happy, and so were his agent and the vice president. And so was I, because after months of false hopes and postponements, at last we had two happy actors and a start date.

Sometimes all the sparring that goes on before the bell is more enervating than the main event itself. Such was the case in my bout with Kathleen Turner. When I first met this extremely talented actress, she was at the start of her Hollywood career and dead keen to play the hooker in the 'New World', low-budget production of *Crimes of Passion*. But that was before her highly successful promotional tour of *Romancing the Stone*, in which, you may remember, she played an intellectual blue stocking.

Well, darlings, let me tell you, by the end of the tour she had turned from an actress playing an intellectual blue stocking into an actual intellectual blue stocking. She played a successful authoress, you may remember, which probably accounts for her being in great demand as a guest of honour with Women's Book Clubs and the like. She was also a particular favourite with the 'Daughters of the American Revolution' I seem to recall. So how could such a paragon of virtue be expected to play a $25-a-trick hooker? The very idea was insulting. Besides she was soon to be married and her fiancé was dead against the idea. So, what happened?

Well, acting on instructions from above, I had to ring her up constantly from Geneva (where I was producing an opera) and sweet-talk her into it, which, for a shy, retiring type like myself, was an extremely cringe-making experience. But I guess it worked, for after a lot of humming and hawing she finally did the movie. Anyway, that's what I firmly believed until I heard a rumour that she had already signed a contract and the production company threatened to sue the pants off her if she reneged on the deal.

Another reason she gave for not wanting to be involved was because the script was anti-American. But I talked her out of that one with an extremely passionate pro-American speech, which gave me no trouble at all as I meant every word of it. For, believe it or not, but for the heavenly intervention of Hollywood, I would never have had a feature film career. No, I've precious little

> **❝** Sometimes all the sparring that goes on before the bell is more enervating than the main event itself. Such was the case in my bout with Kathleen Turner. **❞**

Kathleen Turner as the hooker China Blue acts out a client's fantasy in *Crimes of Passion*.

to thank the Brit film industry for. However, in the event, I lied. *Crimes of Passion* is an extremely anti-American film.

And what of Ms Turner's performance . . . did it suffer because she did the film under duress? Emphatically, NO! Despite everything, it's certainly one of the best of her career, and that's from the lips of the diva herself. In fact, it is one of her favourite roles. And all credit to her. After being reluctant in pre-production, she was professionalism personified during filming and did everything I asked of her, including applying yoghurt to her lips to simulate semen. Come to think of it, there was one exception – she drew the line at swallowing an oyster to give the effect of gulping down a gobful of the white stuff.

So, as you can see, casting can be a bit of a headache – and that's why casting directors were born. They know every last thing you need to know – who's available, how much they cost, who they're sleeping with, and whether or not they have a drug/drink problem. From day one, they give you lists of names for every role of any significance. The best of them give you only a few names per part; the others cover themselves by giving you a virtual telephone book of possibilities. You may as well do it yourself by flicking through *Spotlight*. For that's what it often comes down to when the casting director fails to come up with the right face for the right character.

Spotlight is the *Yellow Pages* of the casting scene – only instead of one enormous tome, there are four of them covering every man, woman and child who can afford to be included. Having said that, it's not to be completely trusted. Human frailty being what it is, one finds many of the photographs are somewhat dated, and more than once I've wondered if the player I've picked from its pages for an audition has sent along their ageing parent instead!

(Opposite) Russell and Twiggy go over the script in *The Boy Friend*.

Listening to the actress' point of view – Russell and Dorothy Tutin on *Savage Messiah*.

No, *Spotlight* is best used as an *aide-mémoire* – a sort of snapshot album to jog the memory and bring back one of the many thousands of thespians plying for hire to the spotlight again. However, there are always exceptions and I have had several surprises when I've seen a new face on a page, called them in for an interview and hit the jackpot. Such was the case with Imogen Millais-Scott – a name totally unknown both to me and my casting director, until we saw her attractive elfin face smiling up at us along with three other hopefuls from a glossy page in *Spotlight*. In the flesh she was a revelation and, for once, didn't look like her own mother. Better still, she looked like her own grandmother – and her own teenage daughter at the same time – not that she had a teenage daughter, of course. And these were just the qualities I needed for the baby doll heroine of Oscar Wilde's *Salome* – who had a head on her shoulders far more mature than her (not so) tender years.

But you can't always go by looks. An attractive Canadian girl was brought to my attention when I was casting around for someone to play Tchaikovsky's sister in *The Music Lovers*. Judging by her performance in a TV *Play of the Month*, she was extremely talented, and more to the point, she actually looked as if she could be related to the actor who was chosen to play the title role. So on the strength of that qualification alone we hired her, and for the first week of shooting all went well. Because of a late start (most films for one reason or another have a late start), we had to do all the exterior sequences first in order to catch the very last sunny holiday Tchaikovsky was ever to spend with his devoted sister on her husband's picturesque country estate.

We were after lyrical, summery images to accompany the highly romantic second movement of the composer's great B-minor piano concerto. And capture them we did, with the happy couple running through silver birch woods, wandering through acres of golden fields of wheat, and rowing in slow-mo across their private lake at sunset. Then came the day when the playback equipment was packed away and we were all set to record our first dialogue scene – in which Natasha pleads with her brother not to return to Moscow, but to prolong their idyllic relationship in the country. Which, to put it frankly, was bordering on the incestuous. It was a dramatic moment and potentially a very moving one.

But as soon as the actress opened her mouth and said: 'Oh Peter, don't go back to Mos-cow, stay here alone with me', in an accent closer to Montreal than Moscow, I seriously thought of jumping in the local lake and ending it all. From the deathly silence that followed my strangled 'cut', in contrast to the usual outburst of sudden chatter, I knew that the rest of the crew were of the same opinion and also wondering, like myself, whether we should cut our losses and recast.

Impossible! We had ten thousand feet of wonderful rushes 'in the can', the weather was on the turn and, although such decisions are not without precedent, the production company would never have stood for it. Instead, I called an early lunch break and rewrote the entire scene, giving Tchaikovsky

all the dialogue. And as he explains why his commitments as a professor at the Conservatoire in Moscow preclude the extension of his holiday, the camera drifts into a close-up of Natasha lying in a hammock silently crying her eyes out – not through ineffable sadness at the loss of her brother to the call of duty, but something far more devastating – the loss of her lines.

Still, she wasn't entirely to blame, poor love – the fault was entirely mine in failing to give her a screen test – with dialogue – for, as I'm afraid I forgot to mention, the part she played in the TV programme which so impressed me, was that of a deaf mute.

> **" ... the camera drifts into a close-up of Natasha lying in a hammock silently crying her eyes out – not through ineffable sadness at the loss of her brother to the call of duty, but something far more devastating – the loss of her lines. "**

Naturally I have never made the same mistake again, although I've had my fair share of casting problems – usually when under pressure from producers to use actors they are particularly keen on. My first experience of this came on *Women in Love*, when, against my better judgement, I was talked into using an actor (whom I felt was miscast) to play Will Brangwen, the father of Gudrun and Ursula, the two women of the title.

He was terrible, or maybe I was terrible in not being able to direct him. Fortunately, all his scenes came during the first week of shooting and after I convinced the producers (who, acting on the evidence of their own eyes, didn't need much convincing) that I could make up for lost time if we moved fast, they concurred and let him go. And in his defence I don't think he was sorry, as he knew for himself it wasn't working. Luckily, Michael Gough, whom I had wanted in the first place, was now available and able to jump on the next train to the Midlands. By great good fortune, the costume fitted perfectly.

However, I wasn't so lucky a few years later when I was pressured to take on an actor I was less than enthusiastic about. This was confirmed on the 'read through' a couple of days before shooting, when it was too late to do anything about it – or was it? Maybe I should have insisted on his departure, but I must admit that is not so easy when the actor is a leading player with a signed contract. Sometimes a second choice can work out surprisingly well, as was certainly the case with *The Music Lovers*.

Impressed with the performance of Alan Bates in the role of the sexually ambivalent schoolteacher who wrestles in the nude with Oliver Reed, in *Women in Love* (more of which later), I had him earmarked for the homosexual composer Tchaikovsky in my following production for United Artists – *The Music Lovers*.

He read the script and was suitably impressed. It was one helluva part, calling for another virtuoso performance of a complex character tormented by his sexual hang-ups. In retrospect, I think that was part of the problem. I guess that Alan didn't want to get typecast as a sexual deviant – heaven forbid! Anyway, after leading me up the garden path for some time, I eventually

learned on the grapevine that he was about to turn me down. He did! Problems with the financiers followed. They'd given the green light to the project on the strength of the casting. Both Alan and Glenda had given very strong performances in *Women in Love*, and the idea of featuring them in their next production under my direction had great appeal, both artistically and financially. Now what?

They'd also been impressed with Oliver Reed in the same film, but baulked at the idea of him tickling the ivories. Besides, I knew full well that he had never played the piano. But apparently United Artist's favourite for the part had and was even something of a virtuoso. I waited breathlessly for the name of the contender and nearly had a heart attack when they announced Richard Chamberlain, better known to me and the rest of the world in those days as Dr Kildare, the glamorous medical consultant in one of the very first in a long line of hospital soaps. I was not happy, but in lieu of any suggestions of my own, agreed to meet him in my agent's office. Yes, we both shared the same agent! This didn't strike me as strange at the time, but then I was a good deal more naïve thirty years ago than I am today.

Russell and family while working on the *Music Lovers*. Centre: Ken and wife Shirley. Children from left to right: Toby, James, Alex, Xavier, Victoria.

Anyway, at the sight of Dr Kildare without his surgeon's robes, I was suitably impressed and even more so when he informed me in all humility that he could strum through the Grieg piano concerto. If he can strum through the Grieg, I reasoned, he could also strum through the Tchaikovsky. I looked at his strong sensitive fingers, so adept at handling surgical saws and scalpelsm, and saw them caressing the keyboard of a Beckstein Grand. So I hired him on the spot. Goodness, gracious me – was I gullible! This guy would have had a problem getting through a one-fingered version of 'Chopsticks'. But I didn't discover this until much later, when I barged unexpectedly into his dressing room where I found him wearing a headset and bashing away on a dummy keyboard.

Yes, he was listening to a tape of the concerto – we'd already recorded - and was miming like mad to the playback. Apparently he'd been doing this in every spare moment since we'd started shooting – knowing he had eight weeks to become a virtuoso, before we were due to shoot his performance of the masterpiece in the last week of the schedule. And as everyone who has enjoyed his stunning performance in the film already knows, he was finger-flicking good.

Even so, the experience taught me to be well on my guard in future and to take an actor's talents according to his C.V. with a large pinch of salt. Nevertheless such is the cunning of the average thespian that they are able to slip through one's defences and pull a fast one. After all, they are 'actors' and learn their survival techniques from a very early age, as I found to my cost on *Mahler*.

Casting the young Gustav was a bit of a problem owing to the fact that he had to ride, swim and play the piano. Most of the boys I auditioned could manage two out of three, but finding a contender who could handle the lot proved difficult. Finally I settled for Gary someone-or-other, who assured me he was fine so far as his athletic abilities were concerned, but was a bit rusty on the piano. I watched him play and thought if I ever made a film of Frankenstein's monster as a young piano prodigy, I need look no further than Gary. However, he read his lines well and looked remarkably like Robert Powell, who was playing Mahler the man. I should have remembered my experience on the Tchaikovsky film and been warned.

So, on the understanding that he practised the piano every day, I hired him. After all, he only had to play scales and I assumed he could manage that with ease. He was a bright boy, keen as Coleman's, and desperate to do the part.

I stopped worrying and got caught up in the hurly burly of pre-production, but still managed to phone him from time to time to see how he was progressing. Gary was never there; he was always down at the baths, according to his mother, who added reassuringly that the piano tuition was coming on fine. I guess I should have smelt a rat – a water rat – but I had far greater problems to sort out and missed the obvious.

What should have been obvious became horrifyingly so on choppy

'Looney Tunes' said Ann-Margaret when she saw this still taken on the set of *Tommy*

William Hurt discusses a scene on *Altered States* with Russell.

Russell gets things moving on *Savage Messiah*.

Derwentwater five weeks later. We had reached the point in the schedule where the young Mahler, wishing to show off to his school chums, attempts to demonstrate that he is as at home in the water as they are, by plunging into the chilly waters of the lake in a foolhardy attempt to swim across it. In the event he only manages a few yards before getting into difficulties and being ignominiously rescued.

So, imagine the scene. There we are, with me and the camera crew in a boat moored a little offshore and young Gary poised on the water's edge in his underwear ready to plunge in, swim into close-up, become exhausted, and start to drown. After a few seconds of this I'd say 'cut', and he'd be hauled safely on board. Everyone knew exactly what was expected of them and we were all keyed up for the take, when Gary's forlorn little voice was caught up by the wind and whipped across the choppy waters towards me.

'Mr Russell,' he shouted through cupped hands. 'I've got a confession to make . . . I lied to you, I can't swim! I can only manage a few strokes.' So that's why he was always down at the baths when he should have been practising the piano, I thought, before shouting back at him:
'Never mind, Gary, just do your best, swim out a few strokes – you needn't even get out of your depth and then pretend to get into difficulties.'
'But Mr Russell, I don't want to, I'm scared.'
'Nonsense! You can do it if you try,' I shouted back with a touch of steel in my voice. 'Ready now – roll camera, action!'

It's amazing how that word 'ACTION' galvanizes the mind. Shout, 'Action' through a loud hailer with command and conviction and you can get a ten-stone weakling to move mountains and pigs to fly. Even our Gary was galvanized sufficiently to wade into the water and take the plunge, for all the world like a cross-channel record breaker. He got all of three yards, started blubbing, and waded shivering and snivelling back to shore. This was disastrous. Defeat was staring us in the face. True, we'd got him in the water and starting to swim, but that was all in long shot. We still needed a few shots in close-up of him swimming and getting into difficulties. And the drowning scene was crucial to the film – we simply had to have it.

'Great, Gary, we've got it,' I shouted. 'Now just jump in a boat and we'll row you out here to discuss the next scene before the light goes.' He wasn't happy, but before he could object an assistant director had bundled him into a boat and started rowing.

'Here, Gary, let me give you a hand,' I said as he was brought alongside. Trustingly he did so, whereupon I sort of lost my balance and poor Gary was hurled into the deep – as both boats pulled away from him like mad and the camera, primed for the crucial moment, purred into action. And what do you know? Gary managed to swim half a dozen strong strokes before giving up the ghost. It was the most convincing drowning scene I have ever seen on the screen. The little bugger couldn't ride a horse either – so we tied him to the saddle and whipped the stallion into a gallop – only kidding! HONEST!

I was going to end the chapter there, but on reading it through, realised with a sinking heart, that I had made one colossal omission – I had not mentioned a single word about the art of acting itself . . . a Freudian slip if ever there was one, I hear you say. Maybe you are right.

I have only seen one director working with actors and that was when I was a member of the cast myself. And I gleaned nothing from the experience that I didn't know already. In fact, it confirmed my belief that what pays off best is simply encouragement and sympathy – unless of course he or she is way off course, when it will be necessary to steer them in the right direction – which by rights should have been done in pre-production, before the cameras even started rolling.

My job is NOT to teach an actor to act, any more than it is my job to tell the D.P. the exposure, or the sound recordist where to position his mike. An actor was taught how to act in drama school and probably has a diploma to prove it. So just let him or her get on with it, coz it's all too easy to confuse the buggers.

I firmly believe that the best way to help an actor is by walking on to the set brimming with confidence and a firm game plan, which you immediately put into action. No shilly-shallying, no indecisiveness, no 'shall we try this' or 'shall we try that'; or before you know it, the actors will be directing the scene themselves and you will be up to your ears in kaka of the equine kind (see Hitchcock).

CHAPTER IV

PRE-
PRODUCTION

Now that you've got your star signed up and the green light has been given, funds start to trickle and you are all set to go into pre-production proper. This is where it starts to get really exciting and the dream begins to turn into reality.

You feel like God about to create the world – for that in fact is what you are about to do. But, praise the Lord, you usually have more than seven days to achieve it; sometimes you have seven weeks, sometimes seven months, sometimes even seven years (as indeed was the case with Sir Dickie and *Ghandi*). But unlike God, you need a little help from your friends.

For unless you are starting off for the very first time (in which case, the very best of British, mate), it generally makes sense to select a crew you know from past experience that you can rely on. But the chances are that your key personnel may not be available, because the day after the 'end of picture party' many of your handpicked crew will be starting a new picture the very next day or the very next week. Whereas you, the director, will have several months ahead of you before you can finally put the picture to bed. Then, by the time you get your next movie off the ground, your favourite technicians could be scattered to the four corners of the earth. And so you start again – which in many ways is no bad thing – horses for courses. Some technicians you find work better in the studio, others shine on location, some are better at highly polished costume drama, others at gritty lowlife stuff. So if you get lucky, you can begin to pick and choose a bit.

The most important relationship you will have is with the producer, who is the man with his hands on the purse strings. He could be the man who owned the project in the first place, or someone he elects to supervise the job for him. He is there to keep his eye on the budget, to ensure the smooth running of the unit and to deal with any unexpected expenses that might arise (and always do). He can turn out to be your best friend or your worst enemy and is often a wolf in sheep's clothing.

So make sure you don't get bitter. Be more specific, I hear you cry. Well, let's think. Let's say you want a particular actor for a particular part and suppose the producer checks him out and finds his fee is higher than the amount in the budget for that particular role – even by a very small sum – all the producer has to do, is throw up his arms and say to the director, 'He just signed for another movie only yesterday, ain't that tough!' – then he'll probably go on to suggest someone a bit cheaper – and not as good.

And this could happen all the way down the line – cast, crew, locations, composers – the lot. Now I'm not saying this is the norm, but it does happen – believe me. On the other hand, most producers I've worked with are gems who will scrimp and save and rob Peter to pay Paul and do whatever it takes to make the director happy, because a happy director is an efficient director. So let's cut the cackle and get on with the crewing up.

> **" Your cameraman comes first – he's 'king of the floor'. If the director is God, then he is the Sun "**

Your cameraman comes first – he's 'king of the floor'. If the director is God, then he is the Sun and all the other departments servicing the movie are lesser luminaries revolving around him. They may not always see it that way, but that's pretty well the reality of it and this is even more so the case in the States, which has a different crewing system to that of Europe. The cameraman – sorry, they prefer to be known as D.P.s (Directors of Photography) – picks his own crew who are answerable only to him.

This usually consists of a clapper/loader or two, focus puller, camera operator and 'grips' (the guy – often a weightlifter, ex-boxer or merchant seaman – who manhandles the camera around, (they can weigh a ton) and fits it on a crane, tripod, or Dolly, and operates that equipment accordingly). The D.P. is generally treated with extreme deference by his crew and is frequently addressed by his forename with the suffix of 'Sir', viz Cecil, Sir.

In the old days they used to live and die in dark homburg hats, camel hair coats, canary-coloured kid gloves, checked bow ties, cavalry twill trousers, and spats worn over brown suede shoes. One I knew even sported a shooting stick. Another wore a monocle fitted with blue glass, but that was back in the days of black and white. Now they mostly wear the obligatory jeans and

Russell stands in for 'Tommy', the rock messiah.

baseball cap. They are lords of all they survey. One very fine cameraman – sorry, D.P. – of my acquaintance has trained his crew to be courtiers.

Wherever he goes, whatever the circumstances, you will find that whenever the lunch break arrives, his private table will be laid – either under the shadiest palm tree, if it be the tropics; or behind the one and only sheltering boulder, if one is on location in the Highlands. And if he and his acolytes are lunching in the tropics, the champagne will be cooling in a silver ice bucket at just the right temperature to his taste; whereas in the northern climes, where the weather is less clement, the Cabernet Sauvignon, having been warmed between the comely thighs of his pretty clapper/loader will be very close to womb temperature, which is exactly how he likes it.

I have often envied him as I have either sweated in the full glare of the sun or shivered on the open heath, as I sipped Perrier water in my paper cup in regions as far apart as Kathmandu and the Isle of Eigg.

Yes, the D.P. is a V.I.P. indeed, as is the director's constant companion – the female he will laugh and fight with, and love and hate for the next . . . for argument sake, let's say ten weeks. Six weeks pre-production and four weeks filming. No, she's not the cute assistant make-up girl who looks like a hot little number well-practised in the art of touching up, but the woman over there in the corner who looks like a bag lady on a bad day. She is your continuity girl, a.k.a. the Script Supervisor. She is the non-marital equivalent of a nagging wife. And since I first started in the industry when most of you were only knee-high to Barry Norman, I must have suffered tongue-lashings from more than a score of 'em and I've still got the scars to prove it.

That was back in the early 1960s, when the continuity girl – sorry, that should read continuity 'lady' – was the female equivalent of a D.P. – both in terms of status and sartorial elegance. Impeccably dressed and coiffed in twinset and pearls, she looked as if she'd just stepped out of the pages of *Vogue* or the hallowed halls of Harrods – and all this at eight o'clock in the morning. Her demeanour was invariably something between a super-efficient chief executive in the city and a high-class call girl. Very businesslike

Russell setting up a shot for *Altered States* as Charles Hald memorizes his lines.

in the day and very discreet at night – in her clandestine affair with a high-flyer in the movie industry. For she rarely had congress with anyone on the crew lower in rank than producer. She was always very self-contained and self-sufficient with her stopwatch, mini-typewriter, folding stool and briefcase containing all her essentials, including The Script and her make-up.

Except for her close relationship with the director, she held herself aloof from the crew who treated her with great respect. But by God, did she know her job! And what exactly was her job? It might be easier to list what her job was not, because it covered so many aspects of feature film production.

Her main concern was the BIBLE, of which she was the chief custodian. And for those not in the know, the BIBLE is the shooting script – which to her was sacrosanct. She would rather go to the stake than allow one word of it to be changed – unless she received a dispensation from the Almighty himself in the shape of the director.

Having said that, it must be admitted that these ladies were generally highly intelligent, well-educated and had a greater understanding of the script than anyone else in the unit. They were thus able to point out weaknesses and inconsistencies that may have escaped even the director himself. Yes, if there were to be script changes they were usually at her suggestion and with her blessing. So it's hardly surprising that a number of these extremely talented ladies went on to become fully fledged producers and made films in their own right, many of which were moderately successful.

Today it's a different story. The continuity girl is very much a girl who is best mates with all the crew – to her it's frequently just a job and not a vocation. And although they're ready, willing and able, they are a totally different breed. Goodbye, twinset and pearls, hello, T-shirt and jeans. Although there are still a few bag ladies about…

Next on the list, in order of importance, is the Assistant Director, who is responsible for organising the troops and ensuring they achieve their daily objective. He's a sort of sergeant major, bless him. Ask anybody who's been in the forces and you will find that they are a much maligned figure, either loved or hated – usually the latter.

It is a difficult job, for he has to be firm but understanding, efficient without being officious. And above all, he has to be respected by his crew, for if he's not . . . then the shoot is going to be a tedious uphill struggle. He's always the bridesmaid, never the bride, the first A.D. – with the accent on 'assistant', for the chances of him becoming a fully-fledged director himself are minimal. In fact, I can't think of a single example.

However, don't get me wrong, a good A.D. is worth his weight in gold and out of the score or so I've worked with, just two stick out in my memory. Number one married my first wife and number two is the proud mother of a bonny bouncing daughter. Yes, I forget to mention, they have female A.D.s now.

But when I started in the business they were as rare as a nun in a monastery. Why, you may ask? Well, I suppose it was simply because back in the bad old days, no painter, chippie, or sparks worth his salt was going to be bossed about by a bit of skirt. For in those far-off days, that is how she would have been viewed. But since the advent of women's lib, things have changed for the better, and ability rather than gender is the main criterion.

Although there is another aspect to the situation worth considering – the domination factor. For let's face it, there's a certain type of male, bless him, who actually likes being dominated by a female – and I firmly believe their numbers are increasing daily. Especially if she is a gorgeous, mini-skirted six footer, with big knockers, sweaty armpits reeking of Chanel No. 5, fabulous legs, a big ass and all-over tan. Yep, she can twist even the most hardened artisan – and believe me, I mean hardened – around her little finger. And when she dances on the pub bar at night, it's clear to see why they'd all bend over backwards for her.

It also comes down to personal relationships. Given a choice with contestants of equal talent, most straight directors would chose a woman. The only risk might be a little friction with the continuity girl, who, as already mentioned, also has a close relationship with the director – rather like the first wife and the chief concubine vying for the favours of the mighty sultan. Yes, some directors do have delusions of grandeur, I'm afraid.[*]

[* See James Cameron's acceptance speech on receiving the Oscar for directing *Titanic*.]

Russell on location in the Lake District on *Rime of the Ancient Mariner* for Granada TV.

(Overleaf) Valentine's Day with Twiggy and some bright young things in *The Boy Friend*.

Oh dear, I've forgotten the Production Designer – who should be top of the list if we're going in order of importance. I can only think I have passed him by because his role is not as obvious as some. He and his team usually work well away from the hustle and bustle of the studio floor in quiet rooms, frequently in distant buildings. Isolation is essential, for his job is a highly creative one developed in what is really an atelier atmosphere, where several talented artists work towards a shared goal.

Lord of all he surveys, the production designer is assisted by an Art Director, whose job it is to translate the P.D's vision into practical plans for the construction of sets and any unique props that have to be especially constructed. He in turn is supported by an army of sketch artists, scenic artists, assistant architects, set dressers, prop-buyers, prop men and women, plasterers, painters, and carpenters. It's a veritable empire, self-contained and answerable only to the top man who is generally held in the highest regard. Unfortunately his role is often underestimated by cinema audiences or, at best, taken for granted.

A recent example springs to mind – *The Matrix*, whose dazzling production values blind one to the banalities of the script. The production designer is the only member of the crew who is there from day one, discussing the overall look of the picture with the director and scouting town and country with him, looking for any locations that may be necessary to the story. Nailing down locations is an all-important priority, for the choice of these will often dictate the style of what is to follow.

On these 'Recces' as they are known in the U.K. (in the U.S. they are known as 'Scouts') comes another member of the crew I have also overlooked – the Location Manager – who has a hand in choosing locations or at least offering up a selection of possibilities – if he's done his homework properly, that is. If you need a country cottage with a thatched roof, he'll know half a dozen. If it's a stately 18th-century mansion you're after, he knows just the job. And if it's a solitary sycamore standing in a field of cows, he knows the very spot.

'But does the field have a slope rising in a Southerly direction?'

'Yes, Guv.'

'And a picket fence all around?'

'Yes, Guv.'

'And is it full of four-leafed clover?'

'Yes, Guv.'

'That's great! Can I see photos please?'

'Yes, Guv, they'll be on your desk first thing tomorrow morning.'

Of course, they never are. True, he may have a fair idea where to find a suitable cottage or stately home and although he hasn't a clue where to find the sycamore in a field of four-leafed clover surrounded by a picket fence, there's no doubt he will spend the next day driving the length and breadth of the county until he finds one, or something pretty close.

Imagine the scene as the location manager appears in the director's office a number of days later.

'Sorry for the delay, Guv, the chemist fucked up, I had to re-shoot the lot all over again – anyway, here they are' – and he plonks a whole stack of contact prints onto your desk, braced for your commentary as you sift critically through them.

'Well these are country cottages alright, but they all seem to have slate roofs.'

'We're in the wrong county for thatch, Guv, but there's one there somewhere, I'm sure.'

'Ah yes, but it has a modern extension with big picture windows.'

'I know, Guv, but if we cut down a tree or two and dress them to camera we can hide that bit and you'll never know.'

'Hm, well, at least this 18th-century mansion looks pretty promising. Did you do a deal with the owner?'

'I tried, Guv, I really did, but he wouldn't play ball, he's had a film unit there before. Still, I thought I'd take a picture or two, anyway.'

'It seems you took thirty-six of them.'

'For reference, Guv. I thought they'd be useful as reference. Now I found your field, but as you see, it's not quite as I remember it.'

'No, I see the sycamore has grown into an oak and judging by the sun, that slope is heading due North.'

'Well it was South according to my compass Guv; I must get it checked. As for the tree, I thought if props could get rid of the acorns you'd hardly know the difference – its OK with the farmer – I slipped him fifty quid.'

'Do you have a receipt?'

'No, not on me, Guv, but I daresay I may be able to find it. But I can positively guarantee it's a field of clover.'

'Hmmm... surrounded by a barbed wire fence.'

'Nothing the art department can't fix in a couple of jiffies – promise, Guv.'

'And the fact that the cattle are not cows but sheep can also be fixed, I'm sure.'

'Piece of cake, Guv.'

Still he did his best and you might be forgiven for thinking he had an impossible task, driving over England looking for something that probably doesn't exist. Except that he doesn't drive all over England – the production manager would never condone it. He works within a radius of fifty miles.

Ah, another new bod – and what does he do? He sees that wages are paid, bills are settled and any day-to-day problems are taken care of. He is responsible to the producers in all matters financial and for the smooth running of the production. And indirectly might even play a key part in the choice of locations.

30049-A-4

Russell working in a freezing, broken-down theatre in Portsmouth while filming *The Boy Friend*.

For as a general rule, all locations have to be within a twenty-five-mile radius of your base, because while you are travelling you can't be filming, and there comes a point where it is just not economic, no matter how desirable a location may be. And if your base can be within the London area (where most of your crew reside) so much the better, because you won't have to put up 60 bodies or so in an expensive hotel, while paying them a per diem. Once again, this can make a big hole in your budget, which can always be spent on more essential items.

Now obviously your choice of base is dictated by the requirements of the script. That you need a lot of office space goes without saying. But you will also need dressing rooms, a make-up area, a camera storage unit, wardrobe space, a production department and a design department. If you need sets built and a sound stage, you might also need a pukka feature film studio, containing every facility you could possibly need, including cutting

(Opposite) Scott Anthony extolling the virtues of Primitive Art in *Savage Messiah*.

Russell directing his son Toby on the set of *Women in Love*. He is watched by Oliver Reed and wife Shirley (back to camera), dressed as an extra.

rooms, viewing theatres, a restaurant to feed your voracious crew – and most importantly, a bar.

Now if you don't need stage space and your film is all on location, you might be able to find a big empty house or deserted factory nearby and service the unit with a collection of mobile homes, Portaloos and caravans that might save you a few pennies, but is far from convenient. I would say go for a studio every time (if you can afford it) – even if you don't need stage space, things will generally run a lot smoother.

There are half a dozen major studios in the London area to choose from and a final choice will come down to the best 'deal' the producer can work out, together with the proximity of the locations required – obviously the closer the better. So we are in our studio and have drawn a 50-mile diameter circle around it, knowing we stand a pretty fair chance of finding the locations we require within that area. It is then we send out our location manager to scout around and give us some choices – so he only has around 400 square miles of highways and byways to cover on his voyage of discovery.

But do not believe for a moment that he is treading virgin territory. One Georgian house he finally leads us to has been used numerous times before – with the departing unit leaving by the back door as the new arrivals are coming in the front. I'm told that to cope with the rush they're seriously thinking of installing a revolving door.

To those in the know, it's quite a game spotting the building in question, as it pops up regularly in cinema and TV in a variety of guises and peopled with a host of posturing actors, some in contemporary dress as in *Peter's Friends*, and others in period schmutter, as in my own *Lady Chatterley* and *Gothic*.

> " Finding locations is fun, and even familiar territory can reveal architectural gems you'd never guess at. "

Finding locations is fun, and even familiar territory can reveal architectural gems you'd never guess at if you hadn't acted on a hunch and taken a peep over that garden wall or driven up that leafy lane.

Yes, it's all going on in pre-production, where there are never enough hours in the day or days in the week as the remorseless six-week countdown gallops by at a rate of knots – when you might be seeing actors in the morning, looking at locations in the afternoon and interviewing potential crew members in the evening. Let's see, who do we still need?

Well, we need a film editor, but that's easy – my son Xavier, who is well versed in my way of shooting, would be my first choice, if he's available! Nepotism, nepotism, do I hear cries of nepotism? Then let me tell you something, he's been working on my films since the age of five (he's now forty-three) – my nepotism goes back a long way.

(Overleaf) Henry VIII and Anne Boleyn as played by Russell and daughter Molly in *Lady Chatterley*.

Which just leaves the sound department, who are frequently treated like

the poor relations. Take the D.P. for instance – after an hour of lighting the set to perfection, he notices the offending shadow of a mike boom, which has only just appeared. He asks the soundman if he can place the boom elsewhere. The soundman tries a new position but is not satisfied with the sound quality. So the D.P. has to try and light out the shadows, which could easily compromise the dramatic effect he is after. No, they are rarely the best of friends. And how many times, when the director is itching to say, 'Action', has the assistant director muttered, 'Still waiting for sound, Guv.'

So what are sound doing? Well, they could be gluing strips of felt on the actors' shoes so they won't clatter and ruin the dialogue, as he runs across the parquet floor in his leather shoes – or even carpeting the floor itself – providing it's out of shot of course.

'Why do you always have to leave this sort of thing to the last moment?' the director might say.

'Because you were rehearsing with the actors on the set till the very last moment,' he might say in protest. That's 'sound' for you – they've always got an excuse ready. Wankers!

Well, I think that pretty well covers the crew, except for all the assistants, secretaries and runners, who are all essential cogs in the machine which constitute the smooth running of the unit. These are chosen by the individual H.O.D.'s (Heads of Department) who always try and get hold of the old reliables they have worked with in the past, year in year out.

So much for the crew. No, it's not – how could I possibly have forgotten the costume designer – a key player if ever there was one. I can only think it comes from being married to one for twenty-five years . . . and talking costumes morning, noon and night. And spending many of my free moments rummaging through mouldy garments on market stalls and searching through miles of dress rails in a multitude of thrift shops. No, the costume designer is crucial to your movie, whether it be ancient or modern.

It is an occupation fraught with problems. If you are shooting a contemporary subject and you are dressing a star off the rail, say, then you have the personal taste of the star to contend with, who will want to wear a garment that makes her look good rather than something that's good for the character she is playing. In which case it pays dividends for the director to go on the shopping spree as a supportive but sobering influence, because the star is more likely to listen to him than the costume designer – no matter how exalted her status.

The problem with period films is that if the costumes have to be designed and made-to-measure, they can easily make the actress look like a clothes horse, whereas they should look lived in and not straight off the clothes hanger. Ideally, one should use the real McCoy unless it is tattered and torn beyond repair. Most such garments are in museums now, but when I started off making films in the 1960s, it was still possible to pick up

Victoria Russell in one of
her many appearances in
Dad's films.

any number of spectacular 1920s flapper dresses with lots of sequins and fringing in most second-hand shops up and down the country, not to mention wonderful Edwardian numbers and a few Victorian and Regency costumes. But the cupboard has long since been bare, so if you are thinking of popping into 'Oxfam' or 'Help the Aged' to pick up a cheap period wardrobe, forget it, unless you are doing something in the postwar period or perhaps the 1930s, in which case you might still get lucky.

But be it ancient or modern, I still think it pays dividends for the director to attend as many wardrobe fittings as possible, be it for a star or a 'walk on', since it gives a player a terrific boost of self-confidence and shows they are working with a caring director who will do his best to make them look good and feel good. And if they look and feel good in front of the camera, the chances are they will act good. Wow, how time flies when you're having a good time – only one week to go and still so much to do.

The week starts off with a production meeting attended by the producer, the director, all the H.O.D.s, and a fair number of fresh faces, including various assistant directors, production secretaries, and not forgetting the gaffer. He's in charge of the lamps and at least one day of the week will be spent visiting all the locations with the D.P. to discuss lighting requirements – but that's jumping ahead. So we choose a day for the lighting recce, then get down to the nitty-gritty. This entails going through the script page by page, line by line, for now is the time to speak or forever hold your peace. This is the moment when things are clarified down to the last detail: from the number of extras required for any one scene, to the number of cherries on a plate.

By the end of the meeting, which usually takes a long morning, everyone has a good idea as to what is expected of them. And not only them, but everyone else – so there will be no future alibis, or cries of 'no one told me' or 'I didn't know'. And it is often only at this late stage that the left hand finally knows what the right hand is doing, and that there are only a few days left to shake on it. 'Then why not hire everyone earlier?' you say. Money, my friend, money!

One day gone and four to go. There are still costumes to be completed and some last-minute alterations to clothes made for an overseas artist, who had to fax his measurements – which may have been accurate once upon a time but invariably turn out to be woefully small. Then there's a final dash around the prop shops; a few more casting sessions; the painting of the sets to keep an eye on; a quick trip to the country to look at a fabulous thatched cottage that has just come to light; camera tests; make-up tests; and finally a readthrough of the script by all the leading players – most of whom are meeting each other for the first time – followed by a buffet lunch, and as far as the director is concerned, a great deal of heart-searching. Now it's sink or swim. Time to get pissed!

CHAPTER V

PRINCIPAL PHOTOGRAPHY

The first day of principal photography is generally a bit of an anti-climax – the fun of foreplay is over and now comes the serious business, which, let's face it, can be a bit of a grind – especially if the script is uninspired, as is frequently the case in the majority of made-for-TV movies that make up the bulk of feature-length films churned out annually on the standard twenty-one day assembly line. For many of the crew, the main thrust of their job is to find a willing sexual partner for the duration of the shoot, and to make sure there is another three-weeker to step into as soon as the director yells, 'clappers on end'. Of course there are still dedicated souls who give their all – way above the call of duty, but they are the exception rather than the rule.

But it wasn't always like that and in the world of the Hollywood Blockbuster, quality and commitment go hand in hand – with time and money no object. I've experienced both ends of the spectrum and, believe me, I know. Enough of that, time to press on and mix with the crew, dropping words of encouragement as they stock up on bulging bacon sandwiches and mountains of black pudding washed down by mugs of a grey liquid masquerading as coffee. The first A.D. sidles up looking glum.

'Morning Guv, bad news I'm afraid. The Land Rover carrying the camera equipment is bogged down in the mud. But not to worry, a tractor is on the way to haul it out.'

In image: `2 3/3 M4 #4 8/ / NAFLEX / MAG 4`

Russell going for just
one more take...

We are on location in the Peak District and it's been a wet week. I nod and go on sipping my coffee and brandy. The make-up girl steps out of the star's caravan, with tears in her eyes.

'Problems?' I ask.

'I've just spent two hours on her makeup and the bitch has just gone and wiped it all off. She wants to do her own.'

'Leave it with me,' I say, 'I'll deal with that one after I've set up the first shot with stand-ins'. In collaboration with the D.P. we settle on a tracking shot, which will take our actors (in search of a missing person) along a mountain path into a sinister cave. And while the crew are setting up I knock on the star's caravan door.

'Yes,' she says.

'It's Ken,' I say. She bids me enter.

I'm prepared for a showdown – her tardiness is going to put us behind schedule.

'Hi Ken,' she says, turning to me with a beaming smile and perfect make-up. 'Good luck love, we're going to have a wonderful shoot, I just know it. Now give me a kiss.' I do so. 'Now what was it you wanted?' she asks innocently.

'Just to wish you all the luck in the world,' I say, kissing her again.

'See you on the set, love,' she gushes as I head for the door.

'Maybe I should fire the fucking make-up girl,' I thought to myself as I walked towards the camera set-up. The trouble was, she was the hairdresser's girlfriend and if she went, both went.

'Sorry Guv,' said the grips, 'we 'aven't enough track to do that shot you wanted; we're short by twenty feet or so.'

'But I ordered fifty feet.'

'Sorry Guv, we've only got thirty. If there's a discrepancy you'd better take it up with the P.M. Sorry!'

'Anyone seen the Production Manager?' I shouted.

'He's off trying to find a tractor,' someone replied.

So here he was, cutting down already, saving money, economising, making me compromise. 'I know I ordered 50 feet of track, I know it.' And we needed that length of track to accommodate the actors' dialogue. Simple solution: cut some dialogue. I sought out the continuity girl and got to work with the blue pencil. Thirty minutes later, thanks mainly to the efforts of the P.M. in finding a tractor, we were ready to rehearse. The actors walked along the mountain path conversing energetically while the

Twiggy and Russell 'waiting for sound' on *The Boy Friend*.

(Overleaf) Julian Sands about to get a manicure in *Gothic*.

camera tracked along with them. We were ready for a take – or were we? No, judging by the look on the operator's face, we weren't.

'Sorry Guv,' he said, 'the lens is all fogged up with condensation, it's the damp mountain air.'

10.03, the continuity girl wrote in her logbook when I finally called action. What would the moneymen make of that when the news was put on their desks in Hollywood the next morning. Scene one, take one, and we were already at least an hour behind schedule. That didn't bode well for the future. Black mark. Excuses are unacceptable and they are such paltry excuses at that, all of which should have been anticipated and provided for.

Worse was to come – the star fell off her bicycle and bashed her face in and no amount of make-up, no matter how carefully applied was going to hide that. We'd have to shoot round her swollen shiner. Even worse, she unexpectedly revealed that she was pregnant – and to my horror it was already beginning to show. If I hadn't been a devout Catholic I would have prayed for a miscarriage.

The male stars (Alan Bates and Oliver Reed) were also promising to be a problem. The nude wrestling scene was coming up. Initially they'd been very gung-ho about it, but as the shooting day drew near their enthusiasm rapidly diminished. One of the contenders complained of a sore ankle and took to limping while the other began to develop a cold and went about sniffing and coughing. Both maladies were completely imaginary despite their best efforts to act out their ailments. At first I didn't take them seriously, but when they both produced doctors' certificates excusing them from stripping off regardless, I ignored their protestations, brushed aside their medical certificates as not worth the paper they were written on, wished them a good evening, and advised them to have an early night, so as to be on set bright and early the following morning, ready for the fray. What I didn't tell them was that I had also scheduled an alternative scene featuring the girls in case the boys dug their heels in and refused to strip off.

The fateful day arrived with everyone poised ready to rush onto the alternative set in case our two unwilling protagonists should really chicken out. But dead on the stroke of 8.30 a.m., they both strode into the baronial hall, where the fight was due to take place, whipped off their dressing-gowns without demur and stood there as naked as the day they were born – proud as peacocks. So for the rest of the day and most of the next we shot the controversial wrestling scene that made screen history – without any sign whatever of a sore ankle or a single nasal sniff. Who or what had worked this seemingly major miracle?

Well, when it was all over, I finally found out. The person responsible was the stand-in for the more macho of the two actors. According to his

> The fateful day … they both … whipped off their dressing-gowns without demur and stood there as naked as the day they were born – proud as peacocks.

testimony, he had cajoled them into joining him for a drink at the local pub in order to drown their depression and further strengthen their resolve to stand firm in their decision. Not usually the best of friends, the alcohol mellowed them into becoming quite chummy and by the time their bladders reached bursting point, they staggered off to the outside loo, giving each other mutual support. And it was much to their mutual relief that as far as their manhood was concerned, there wasn't much to choose between them. It had all been a question of 'size' and male vanity. Having said that it has to be admitted that one of the contestants cheated by giving nature a helping hand just before every take. Next day there was bad news from the labs – the negative of one of the takes had developed a scratch during processing, but the good news was that it could be polished out.

Well, those are some of the trials and tribulations that come with filming. They don't come every day, thank God. But all these setbacks and many, many more have happened to me at one time or another during my career, and are just a few of the problems that one might come up against before the ever-welcome arrival of the end-of-picture party, which never comes a day too soon and more often than not leaves the director, for one, bloody but unbowed.

CHAPTER VI

POST PRODUCTION

N ow comes the calm after the storm. Suddenly the director is alone well, almost. The producer, the P.M. and a handful of the office staff are still around and of course so is the gang in the cutting rooms, which comprises the picture editor, the sound editor and their various assistants. It is with these lads and lasses that the director will spend the next six to eight weeks – unless he is working on a really big one bulging with special effects, when he could be looking over the editor's shoulders for up to a year or more – as was my own particular case with *Altered States*.

This was chock-a-block with optical effects, some of which needed to pass through twenty-seven optical processes to get the special effect required – any one of which could have malfunctioned. And the snag was that there was no way of checking until the final pass was developed and printed, when, after weeks of work, you at last found out if you'd got lucky or were doomed to start all over again, having learned from your mistake(s). Of course, that was way back in the pre-digital days of the early 1980s.

Nowadays when the most sophisticated optical effects are created electronically and can be checked every step of the way, there is far less likelihood of error. All the same, the process is extremely time-consuming and consequently doesn't come cheap. But although some of the visual effects in *Altered States* still look pretty stunning today, they look pretty basic compared to what is achievable at the present time – think of *The Matrix*; think of Oliver

(Overleaf) Dance of the 'sugar plum fairies' in the *Music Lovers*.

Reed raised from the dead in *Gladiator*, to appear in two more scenes, while turning in his grave in rural Ireland.

> " I like editing; it's very much a hands-on process, somewhat akin to the art of the potter, who starts off with a mass of raw material and ends up shaping it into a polished object, pleasing to the eye. "

I like editing; it's very much a hands-on process, somewhat akin to the art of the potter, who starts off with a mass of raw material and ends up shaping it into a polished object, pleasing to the eye. Basically, I have edited my film before even shooting a foot of it. Edited in my head, that is.

As everyone knows, a film script is broken down into scenes, each of which advances the story. Some are long, some are short, some are slow in tempo, some are fast, some are tense, others relaxed – and analogous to musical forms like a classical symphony, which in the course of its journey of discovery and revelation might encompass all these moods and expressions. For example, take my film on Mahler, which I composed in rondo form, meaning: original theme, new material, original theme, new material etc. (A, B, A, C, etc.). In this instance, the A theme represented Mahler's long journey by train back to his home (after a tiring conducting tour), interspersed with flashbacks of his journey through life.

To me, structure is an immensely important element in filmmaking, where the nature of each scene dictates its own structure and development in relation to each succeeding scene. To swap analogies for a moment, it's also akin to bridge building.

It is common practice for many directors (in fact it's an old Hollywood tradition) to break down a scene into long shot, mid shot and close-ups. This might give maximum choice in the editing process, but it's a very mechanical device devoid of imagination.

Music doesn't work with options; it's a precise science. I firmly believe that each scene has its own particular dynamic which in itself dictates the manner in which it should be approached – anything from a single choreographed shot, where the camera and the actors move around each other like dancers, to a series of staccato shots rattling off like a machine gun. The trick is to make the right choice. And that can be achieved before one frame of the film is exposed, if the director has done his homework. If this can be achieved, then the potentially tricky business of editing can be a simple matter of selecting your preferred take and simply joining it on to the previous one.

That's the ideal theory, though I must confess it rarely works out that way, which is why one generally takes a few cutaway shots that could get one out of trouble. Reaction shots are often a godsend and are ideal for shortening a scene that is outstaying its welcome, or in cutting out or cutting down an acting performance that is not up to standard.

There is also another hitch to my theory – for whereas a composer can work through his score in continuity, most directors shoot out of continuity. There are a variety of reasons for this, which become obvious the moment you think about it. For instance, if your opening and closing scene are set in the Outer Hebrides, while the rest of your script is set in London . . . well you are not going to make two expensive excursions when you can do it in one, are you? Similarly if you have a costly actor who only appears in the opening and closing scenes – well you are not going to keep him under contract for six weeks when you can, say, get rid of him in six days.

You can see the problem, can't you? You have to guess how your actor's character is going to develop in the middle section so that it will dovetail into his performance in the grand finale. Ah, you might say, it's all there in the script – it's obvious. But then I might point out that films have an annoying habit of developing a life of their own, resulting in unpredictable shifts of character and even plot.

That was one great advantage I found when directing opera; not only do you rehearse each scene in continuity, you even have the finished soundtrack to work to, where emotions are orchestrated and tempo is timed to the precise tick of a metronome. So if it's *Madame Butterfly*, and you have adequate singers, and an OK conductor who doesn't interfere with the staging of the production, then you can pretty well guarantee that you have a hit on your hands.

Films are another matter. With films nothing is guaranteed – no matter how big the investment. Think of *What Dreams May Come*, think of *The Postman*, think of . . . no I'd better not say it, I might get sued. But I've personal knowledge of a recent potential turkey that was turned into a Golden Goose by the miraculous skills of a brilliant editor of my acquaintance, brought on board to save a sinking ship – if you'll pardon my mixed metaphors. Yes, an editor can make or break your movie.

So you start the first day of post production by fine-tuning your film, because by now, your editor should have a rough cut to show you. For every day (more or less) during the shooting, you have both viewed the rushes together, selected the best takes and discussed how they should be assembled. However, in case such a get-together is just not possible (the director may be away on location for instance), the editor always has an updated copy of the continuity girl's detailed script to fall back on.

And while the editor continues to trim and polish according to the director's notes, throughout post production the man himself is engaged in other activities of a kindred nature. Footsteps, post-sync, music, to name but three.

Have you ever noticed that on most TV soaps and news items you rarely hear the sound of footsteps? There is a very simple reason – the microphone is usually pointing at the subject's mouth rather than their feet. 'So what?' you say. To which I reply: on the small screen it doesn't matter when feet of all sizes are reduced to a few millimetres, but on the big screen where they can be magnified to ten times normal size, the virtual absence of any sound accompanying these giant plates of meat would be sorely missed.

> " . . . an editor can make or break your movie. "

(Overleaf) Not exactly 'Swan Lake'. Ex-Royal Ballet star Christopher Gable partners Twiggy in a dance number from *The Boy Friend*.

'I could be happy with you, if you could be happy with me'... Russell rehearsing Twiggy for a recording in *The Boy Friend*.

So they are re-created in the recording studio where a team of highly skilled technicians, eyes glued to the screen, march in time to the silent image they are following and bring it to life. And what is more, they do it on the correct surface, whether it be grass, gravel, sand or snow – for hidden under trap-doors in the studio floor are a variety of surfaces to cover most demands.

But if this is beginning to sound like a foot fetishists' paradise, it's time to relate that they also recreate every other sound on the screen that may not have been picked up in the original recording – from a coffee mug being put down on a counter in a café, to a skull being crushed by a heavy object – where whacking a fresh Savoy cabbage with a hammer can give a spine-chilling effect. Post-synchronisation is often produced in the same studio – usually a small room with a screen, padded walls, and a big glass window looking onto a sound-proofed recording booth where the engineer gets the new sounds down on tape – later to be transferred to magnetic film and run in perfect synchronisation with the picture.

This can be necessitated for a variety of reasons. For instance, say you are shooting a period subject outside a stately home and a 747 flies overhead in the middle of the take. Apart from being anachronistic it would probably drown the actors' dialogue. The process can also be used to improve an acting performance or change it altogether by using a different actor, as I have had occasion to do a couple of times in the past.

Most films need music – they always have done – since long before the introduction of the human voice in fact, as I discovered for myself at the age of 12, when I gave home movie shows in Dad's garage in Southampton during the Blitz, in aid of the Spitfire fund. Born the year Al Jolson made screen history by singing 'Mammy' in *The Jazz Singer*, I had never set eyes on a silent film until my parents gave me a Pathescope Ace home movie projector as a Christmas present, together with a selection of short subjects ranging from Charlie Chaplin to *Felix the Cat* – none of which had a soundtrack.

Neither did the feature films on offer in the Pathescope catalogue that I was able to hire, once I'd fixed extension arms to my little toy in order to accommodate bigger spools. These included masterpieces by the great German director Fritz Lang such as *Metropolis* and *Siegfried* that ran for well over an hour. Even at that tender age, I realised that to expect an audience accustomed to talkies to sit on their backsides for that length of time listening to the clatter of the projector, the drone of Nazi bombers, the crack-crack of anti-aircraft fire, and the crump of falling bombs would be adding insult to potential injury.

This time it was a birthday present that proved a hit – in the shape of a 12-inch shellac record containing a couple of orchestral marches. On the first side was a heroic march by Edward Grieg and on the flip side, a modern one by Arthur Bliss. I played these alternatively on my wind-up gramophone throughout the show and gradually came to the conclusion that as an accompaniment to the Teutonic knight Siegfried slaying the fire-breathing dragon, the Grieg was superb; whereas the march by Bliss, especially composed for a sci-fi film, added real punch to Fritz Lang's *Metropolis*, which was also set in the future. It was an invaluable lesson that was to shape my future career; not only in my series of films on classical composers, but also in works of imagination.

And to insert a nostalgic note for a moment, I have to confess that some of my happiest memories involve those shows in Dad's garage, where the irony of the situation – in which the sons of Siegfried rained down fire from above, as their heroic Aryan ancestor destroyed that evil fire-breathing dragon, totally escaped me. But then as the great Isadora Duncan once said to Comrade Stalin, 'Art knows no frontiers.'

To say that music can make or break a film would be going too far perhaps, but the right score can certainly enhance its impact. Just try turning off the sound next time the shower scene in *Psycho* hits the TV screen, and you will quickly see what a flat, boring bit of filmcraft it is once deprived of Bernard Herrmann's hair-raising score. Alas, his breed appear to have gone for good, along with that great band of refugees who ended up in Hollywood just prior to World War

> **❝** . . . try turning off the sound next time the shower scene in *Psycho* hits the TV screen, and you will quickly see what a flat, boring bit of filmcraft it is once deprived of Bernard Herrmann's hair-raising score.

II: names like Korngold, Steiner and Waxman. However, I readily admit there are undoubtedly some talented names knocking around today – such as Dan Davies who produced an absolute knockout score for *The Matrix*.

The problem with commissioning a score is that you never know what the composer might come up with – no matter how talented he may be. Take Georges Delerue for instance – remember his music for *Jules et Jim* – fabulous! He also did a great job on my first feature film, *French Dressing*. Some folk thought his score was the best thing about the movie, and maybe they were right. But when I engaged him for a repeat performance on *Women in Love*, I had to junk half of everything he wrote. Trying to be serious, he ended up being turgid. Serves me right for hiring a foreigner for such an innately English subject.

I should have learned my lesson from the Ealing Comedies, scored by another talented Frenchman – Georges Auric. Heard in isolation on CD, this is music of a high order; but when seen in conjunction with the pictures it has no connection whatsoever. Maybe he was a friend of the producer.

On many occasions I have edited my films to a piece of existing music lifted from a recording, which through trial and error eventually produced the particular effect I was after. But the trouble with this particular practice is that it is difficult for your jobbing composer not to produce a substandard version of the masterpiece in question. Then why not use the original masterpiece? Because the copyright fee could cost you a fortune – unless the music is out of copyright of course, as was the case in my films on Tchaikovsky and Mahler. And there's not a composer alive who's the equal of that dynamic duo.

Anyway, however you accomplish it, with your music recording in the can you are ready for the big moment – the moment you go into the dubbing theatre to mix all your diverse sounds together and end up with the master track to your picture, which has now reached its final cut – or has it? Mixing the picture can take anything from two days to two months depending on budget and complexity. And it's a thrilling moment when the results of months of blood, sweat, toil, and tears finally come together – what an orgasm!

At various times during the sound dub the director has to sneak away to the labs to supervise the grading of his picture. This involves colour corrections – making scenes that are underexposed a little brighter and scenes that are overexposed a little darker. And also to check out any optical work he deems necessary – the object being to marry the perfect picture to the perfect sound. This is known as the answer print and although there is usually no problem with the sound, several passes are usually required before a satisfactory print is achieved. For this process is by no means an exact science – being prone to temperature, chemicals and human error – a problem which will cease to be once digital tape takes over from crummy old celluloid.

And now we have come to the time when the director reaches for his knuckle-duster, because invariably he is about to have a fight on his hands.

CHAPTER VII

PREMIERE

Very few directors have final cut. Kubrick did, Spielberg probably does and a handful of others. My contracts have usually allowed me three cuts and three previews. And in case this phraseology is a little obscure, let me explain a process that has become more or less standard procedure.

In the olden days, when a director showed his finished film to the company executives – who were usually few in number and ran their company like a small family business – it was usually an informal get-together over lox and bagels for a civilised discussion in which they aired any concerns they might have regarding the director's sacred offering. Maybe it was too long, they might venture, maybe there was a scene or two that didn't quite work and they might suggest, with due deference, a few changes which the director might hopefully consider.

But sometimes the box office receipts threw doubt on these highly subjective decisions and it was felt by the execs that if the audience had also been consulted, then maybe a financial disaster could have been averted. And so the sneak preview was born, whereby an unreleased movie was shown to an audience, unconditioned either by publicity or reviews, who were requested to answer a questionnaire before leaving the cinema. Their comments were then analyzed and generally acted upon.

This would result in the director being requested to make a number of changes that would, theoretically, increase the film's general appeal and, more importantly, increase its box office potential. Sometimes the director would go along with this edict and sometimes he would fight it. I've done both, but even when strongly opposed to any changes, have reluctantly done a few cosmetic cuts just to keep the peace, so to speak. The film would then be shown again and the process repeated; and then just once more for luck. And then with the terms of his contract fulfilled, the company was free to take the director's final cut and do with it as it wished – cutting it to ribbons, if it felt it could make more money out of it by so doing.

But now, even that face-saving chimera has gone – at least for blokes like me. Too time-consuming and too expensive. Instead, we have pages of directives – drop this scene, shorten that scene, swap this sequence for that sequence, and change a whole lot of dialogue. Anonymous commands from a faceless committee of soft drink salesmen with a voice that, no matter how ill-informed, has to be obeyed. THEY know what is best for the public and will make damned sure it's rammed down its throat – hard!

However, although this is becoming the norm with made-for-TV movies, it is not always the case with staple Hollywood fare – as I know from personal experience with *Crimes of Passion*, a black comedy I made in Hollywood, featuring Tony Perkins and Kathleen Turner. Because it was a little bit 'off the wall' and a touch kinky, the financiers decided to preview it in San Francisco, which is pretty liberal-minded in such matters.

The audience seemed to like it – except for the ending, which finished on a note of ambiguity, which left many of them feeling dissatisfied and confused. So, there was this mad preacher in drag, dying in the arms of a hooker while the hero looked on in compassion. 'What happened next?' they wanted to know, 'did the hero shack up with the hooker, with whom he'd fallen in love, or did he go back to his dreary wife and kids?' Well, to me, that didn't matter a toss, because that was a different story – but to the audience it DID matter. And because of this, they only gave the movie a 65% rating. Something had to be done to improve that rating and send the viewers away happy. The solution was simple and – equally important – cheap!

The film had started with the hero in a group therapy session (with a few out-of-focus actors in an otherwise empty room), so I thought it would be quite neat and tidy to end it in the same way. So we get our hero to sit in the same chair under the same lamp with the same anonymous faces in the background and say:
'I guess you're all wondering what happened to the hooker and me. Well, we decided to shack up together – then we went home and fucked our brains out.' Result – a hearty laugh and a happy audience that sent the ratings up to 80% and the prospect of greatly improved profits at the box office. Even so, it doesn't always work out as amicably as that, as the old scars on my back can testify. ' Nuff said!

That said we are now on track for the premiere and as the great day approaches, so the publicity machine, which has been coasting along for some time now, shifts into top gear and is given full throttle. Frequently, mini in-house movies begin to flood the TV networks extolling the virtues of the product, peppered by sound bites from the stars, saying it's the greatest film they've ever done and lauding cast, crew and content to the skies. And never forget that most of those involved are in for a tidy percentage of the profits – just in case you're in danger of allowing yourself to be conned.

Then there are live TV interviews, radio interviews, newspaper and magazine interviews – for those involved in its non-stop merry-go-round of lies, lies, lies – until the limos roll up into Leicester Square or Hollywood Boulevard or wherever, to flickering flashlights and screaming crowds. Then comes the movie . . . and what an anti-climax that can be. What a disappointment, and I'm not necessarily talking about the film itself, but its cinematic presentation.

Personally, I've had more than my fair share of first night disasters, but as they evoke painful memories they are best forgotten. I'll let just one example suffice to prove my point. It happened at the premiere of *Billion Dollar Brain* – my first big-time movie.

I was sitting in the front row of the dress circle next to the film's producer Harry Saltzman (of James Bond fame) when suddenly, on the changeover from one projector to the other at the start of reel three, the picture popped onto the screen without sound and we were back to the era of the 'silents' once more – without the benefit of music or subtitles.

'This can't last,' I thought to myself, 'the projectionist is bound to notice and do something about it'. And I knew there was nothing wrong with the print, because we'd rehearsed the show in the morning. But as the agonizing seconds turned into excruciating minutes and the slow handclapping began I somehow overcame the slow paralysis creeping over me, sprang to my feet and went in search of an usherette.

'Where's the projection box?' I shouted to a dark silhouette above the growing hubbub of protest.
'The what?' she replied.
'The place where they show the films.'
'Search me,' she snapped, 'you'd better ask the commissionaire.'

Tearing down the stairs two at a time, I found him in the foyer chatting up the refreshments girl. I repeated the question. Stunned, he stammered a reply that I doubt you will believe.

'Straight out the swingdoor, Guvnor, down the first alleyway on your right, up the fire escape and across the roof to what looks like a brick shithouse – and give four raps for admittance.' And as I ran like fury to the swing doors, his final words echoed in my ears. 'Make sure it's four knocks or they won't let you in – vandalism.'

Two minutes and four knocks later, I was finally admitted to the inner sanctum by an astonished, ageing projectionist who was too surprised to talk.

'Sound!' I screamed at him. 'There's no fucking sound!' He took the news with surprising calm.

(Overleaf) Michael Caine takes Françoise Dorléac for a ride in *Billion Dollar Brain*.

'I thought it was a bit quiet for a Bond film,' he said, confusing his Saltzman heroes, before slowly putting down the girlie magazine that had been occupying his mind and flicking a switch, which mercifully restored the sound. Two men in smart Saks of 5th Avenue suits now hit the scene. I recognized them as company execs.

'What happened?' they said in unison.

'There was a blip on the automatic changeover,' said the projectionist and left it at that.

'So what are we going to do?' I said. 'We've lost nearly six minutes of important plot development; the audience won't have a clue what's happening.'

'How long will it take to rewind and start the reel again?' barked one of the execs.

'Give or take a minute, I'd say five minutes,' mused the projectionist.

'More like ten,' I mumbled.

'That's suicide,' said the other exec, 'we'll have a riot on our hands.'

He was right. So, somewhat shattered we left the film to churn on, crossed the roof, went down the fire escape, up the alley and back into the cinema, passing several disgruntled patrons on their way out. What a night . . . and it wasn't over – worse was to come, over which I will draw a veil lest I am tempted, as I relive the debacle in my mind's eye, to cut my own throat.

Oh dear, what a downbeat note to end on. But that is not the end for most directors – because there's always the next movie to look forward to, unless, like poor me, you are considered to be unbankable. But cheer up and never say die – hope is at hand.

CHAPTER VIII

BACK TO THE FUTURE

S itting in my idyllic garden in the heart of the New Forest, basking in the summer sun and the scent of roses, watching sky-blue dragonflies skim across the lily-covered pond and waiting for the phone to ring – a typical day in the life of an unemployed but compulsive film maker.

If only I had been a painter or a composer, I could do wonders simply with a pencil and a sheet of blank paper. But as you have seen, a filmmaker needs more – he needs a crew of fifty, a ton of equipment and five million dollars . . . an impossible dream for someone who has made more flops than hits, and at the age of seventy-three is considered way over the hill. Why not face it: so far as the commercial film world was concerned, I was all washed up. Maybe I should buy myself a cheap camera and keep a video journal of my daily life called 'Diary of a Has-Been'.

I chuckled to myself and dismissed the idea in favour of a walk through the forest with 'Nipper', an old English black-and-tan toy terrier – my constant companion. But on the walk, accompanied by a little Vaughan Williams on my personal stereo, the idea persisted. Did I really need a big crew and a big budget to make a movie? After all, I'd launched myself on my directing career with a film I made for four hundred pounds and the help of a few friends. It was a religious fantasy called *Amelia and the Angel* and proved to be my passport to the prestigious BBC Art's programme *Monitor,* where I worked for many years producing a series of prize-

On location in Finland, where
it's cold, for *Billion Dollar Brain*.

winning drama documentaries, which in turn opened the door to the world of feature films.

My mind went back to Emma and Marie Aflixion, a couple of remarkable girls I'd encountered at the Edinburgh Festival nearly a year ago. We met on a chat show where they invited me to their presentation of a personal selection of films from the 'Underground Cinema' – of which I'd never heard. Most of the nine films on view impressed me. Ranging in duration from one to ten minutes they covered a wide range of techniques and subject matter. The sexual adventures of Ken and Barbie in a domestic aquarium were as funny as they were bizarre, while a cartoon showing a wolfman's voyage to the moon was a haunting, mind-blowing trip in more ways than one.

The memory of it all inspired me. The majority of the offerings were the dedicated work of lone individuals beavering away in attics and backyards – why shouldn't I have a bash myself in the limitless confines of my thatched cottage? I decided to bite the bullet, bought myself a video and wrote a script.

Deciding that 'Diary of a Has-Been' was a contradiction in terms of what I wanted to pursue, I went for something more in keeping with an old Columbus off to discover a brand new world – for that is what the camcorder experience proved to be.

For years I'd listened to film buffs extolling the virtues of celluloid over tape, but as I'd always suspected this just wasn't so. OK, so film may have a wonderful, subtle transparency, but tape has a bright compulsive in-yer-face richness of colour and a unique ability to jump out of the screen and hit you – bang! But in the end it's the quality of the content and how it's handled that really matters. Since old habits die hard, I decided on a biopic based on a brief newspaper article that caught my eye one day, telling the story of a defrocked priest who was killed by a lion while sharing this ferocious beast's cage and preaching about Daniel in the lion's den.

It was an ambitious subject and I soon began to wonder if I had bitten off more than I could chew. And I'm sure it would have proved thus but for the selfless efforts of my family, some friends in my village and the two indefatigable girls from the underground. They all rallied round providing their services gratis or, if they had to travel down from town, the price of a return ticket and either a champagne picnic in my garden – where most of the action took place – or if they were staying for more than a day, an early morning cup of tea, bed and breakfast, lunch, evening meal, and as much booze as they could handle.

By the time shooting was over, along with the endless washing up, catering and laundering, I was still only halfway through the instruction manual of my state of the art videocam – but thankfully everything looked fine. Now confronted by a black box called 'Casablanca', which I am told is a Pandora's

Box of editing marvels, I am poised over its extensive manual ready to master the magic spell that will bring this pile of high-tech wizardry to life.

As I view the rushes I am struck by the ambitious nature of the project and how relatively easy it was to produce. The most difficult thing to get right was the script and I can't state how important that is – no matter what your budget. And I didn't feel I could get the script right until I had cast the actor playing the part of our hero, the Rector of Stiffkey.

Let me elaborate a little of his story, which took place during the 1920s and 30s of this century. The Reverend Harold Davidson was a happily married man with four children who, after taking the service at his local church every Sunday, caught the next train to London and spent the rest of the week 'saving fallen women' before returning home late Saturday night.

Eventually he was accused of hanky-panky, brought to trial by an ecclesiastical court, found guilty, defrocked and stripped of his living. He spent the next five years ensconced in a barrel, protesting his innocence. Run out of Blackpool for vagrancy, he joined a freak show in Skegness, and in order to raise funds for an appeal against an unjust verdict, agreed to appear in a lion's cage, preaching the story of Daniel, where, sadly, he was mauled to death.

Hardly the stuff of a shoestring budget, perhaps, but where there's a will there's a way. I advertised in *The Stage* for vicars and tarts willing to appear gratis in an underground film. The venue for the audition was a café at a main line railway station. How the commuters must have wondered at the preponderance of men of the cloth and women of the street on that particular morning in May. Perhaps they thought a religious convention had hit town . . . anyway, although there were several women who would have passed as prostitutes, the potential padres were a most unholy bunch. So we drew a blank there, which was a bit of a setback.

Age was also a problem – Davidson died at the age of 56, although I planned to start his story much earlier, in his childhood. In fact, that posed no problem at all, as I had already earmarked my seven-year-old son Rex for that crucial role. But for Davidson the man, I needed an actor of extraordinary talent and I didn't have one. The phrase, 'if you pay peanuts you get monkeys' came to mind and I wasn't even prepared to pay peanuts, because the golden rule of the underground is 'get it for free with a lot of goodwill' and that is what I was aiming for. There were a couple of actor friends I could have called upon, but they were comedians and I was determined NOT to turn the story into a Benny Hill romp.

Fortunately, I soon realised the obvious. If a man lives in a barrel, all you have to do is find the right barrel, and as Little Jimmy, as he was known, was only five foot, three inches small, you didn't need that big a barrel. But you needed a barrel with a bunghole through which the reverend could communicate with the outside world. With that hurdle jumped, I was off to the races.

More meetings were held in the café that had become our official

Russell whistling for inspiration at one of his favourite locations – the Lodore Falls in the Lake District.

(Overleaf) Russell with Barry Lowe – actor, location manager, property master and crowd-casting director – on the set of Russell's first underground movie, *Lion's Mouth*.

production office, complete with mobile phones and plenty of chilled Italian plonk. And in next to no time we had a script inspired by the 'Rosebud' scenario, which everyone on nodding terms with *Citizen Kane* will be familiar with. Take a dying man's last words as the starting point in putting together the jigsaw puzzle of his life and take it from there. And since the last reported words of Davidson were, 'Make sure you make the late night extra,' it follows that a local reporter from the *Skegness Sentinel* would be the logical choice to put together the pieces.

The role of cub reporter Josephine Heatherington was of key importance and here my daughter Victoria, who was helping out in her professional capacity as costume designer, introduced me to an actor friend who was willing to sacrifice a fee in return for the kudos of appearing in Ken Russell's first underground movie. Fortunately for me, as things turned out she wasn't the only one. And it goes without saying that the two girls who introduced me to the underground should also appear – as a couple of tarts with golden parts.

The rest of the cast was made up of local talent – some of which I'd discovered while doing a documentary on the English folk song. One such luminary, the bearded Barry Lowe, also became the location manager and took care of casting as well – even to the extent of talking twenty-five extras into hiring their own costumes for the one and only crowd scene. He also extracted a variety of crucial props from local tradesmen at the simple cost of a credit. But possibly our greatest coup was getting the classical chart-toppers, 'The Mediaeval Babes' to appear as prostitutes paying their respects to the reverend in the all-singing, all-dancing finale in the local cemetery.

All in all, we were one big happy family and here, in true Hollywood tradition, I'd like to pay special tribute to my artist son Alex, not only for appearing as the 'Angel of Death', but also for constructing a variety of essential props, accompanying me around the local thrift shops to haggle over the price of period costumes, and handling the camera whenever I was foolhardy enough to take to acting.

Already we are planning our next epic – a full-length feature called *The Fall of the Louse of Usher*. This is a project I have consistently tried to set up over a period of at least ten years. It has gone through many stages of development, from a multi-million dollar blockbuster to be shot in Hollywood to a (more or less) no budget underground epic to be shot in my back garden, conservatory and garage.

Much of the music for this black comedy update of Poe's classic tale has been written and key characters cast (I myself am playing the mad psychiatrist Dr. Calihari). We are already planning for our premiere – on the Internet. For therein lies the future for the likes of me and everyone else out there with a video camera, a few willing friends, and a burning desire to topple the status quo and make history.

NOT THE END

KEN RUSSELL'S FEATURE FILMS

FRENCH DRESSING (UK, 1964, 86 MIN)

Production Company:	Kenwood
Director:	Ken Russell
Producer:	Kenneth Harper
Photography:	Ken Higgins
Screenplay:	Peter Myers, Ronald Cass, Peter Brett
Music:	Georges Delerue
Cast:	James Booth, Roy Kinnear, Marisa Mell, Bryan Pringle

BILLION DOLLAR BRAIN (UK, 1967, 111 MIN)

Production Company:	Lowndes
Director:	Ken Russell
Producer:	Harry Saltzman
Photography:	Billy Williams
Screenplay:	John McGrath (based on the novel by Len Deighton)
Music:	Richard Rodney Bennett
Production Designer:	Syd Cain
Cast:	Michael Caine, Oscar Homolka, Françoise Dorléac, Karl Malden, Ed Begley

WOMEN IN LOVE (UK, 1969, 130 MIN)

Production Company:	Brandywine
Director:	Ken Russell
Producer:	Larry Kramer
Photography:	Billy Williams
Screenplay:	Larry Kramer (based on the novel by DH Lawrence)
Music:	Georges Delerue
Editor:	Michael Bradsell
Production Designer:	Ken Jones
Choreographer:	Terry Gilbert
Costume Designer:	Shirley Russell
Cast:	Alan Bates, Oliver Reed, Glenda Jackson, Jennie Linden, Eleanor Bron, Alan Webb, Vladek Sheybal, Catherine Wilmer, Sarah Nicholls, Sharon Gurney

THE MUSIC LOVERS (UK, 1970, 123 MIN)

Production Company: Russfilms
Director: Ken Russell
Producer: Roy Baird
Photography: Douglas Slocombe
Screenplay: Melvyn Bragg (based on the novel, *Beloved Friend* by CD Bowen and Barbara von Meck)
Music Director: André Previn
Cast: Richard Chamberlain, Glenda Jackson, Christopher Gable, Max Adrian, Isabella Telezynska, Maureen Pryor, Andrew Faulds

THE DEVILS (UK, 1971, 111 MIN)

Production Company: Russo
Director: Ken Russell
Producer: Robert H. Solo, Ken Russell
Photography: David Watkin
Screenplay: Ken Russell (based on the play by John Whiting and the novel *The Devils of Loudun*, by Aldous Huxley)
Music: Peter Maxwell Davies
Production Designer: Derek Jarman
Cast: Vanessa Redgrave, Oliver Reed, Dudley Sutton, Max Adrian, Gemma Jones, Murray Melvin, Michael Gothard, Graham Armitage

THE BOY FRIEND (UK, 1971, 108 MIN)

Production Company: MGM
Director: Ken Russell
Producer: Ken Russell
Photography: David Watkin
Screenplay: Ken Russell (based on the play by Sandy Wilson)
Editor: Michael Bradsell
Production Designer: Tony Walton
Choreographer: Christopher Gable, Terry Gilbert, Gillian Gregory
Costume Designer: Shirley Russell
Cast: Twiggy, Christopher Gable, Moyra Fraser, Max Adrian, Bryan Pringle, Catherine Wilmer, Murray Melvin, Georgina Hale, Sally Bryant, Vladek Sheybal

SAVAGE MESSIAH (UK, 1972, 103 MIN)

Production Company:	Russ-Arts
Director:	Ken Russell
Producer:	Ken Russell
Photography:	Dick Bush
Screenplay:	Christopher Logue (based on the novel by HS Ede)
Music:	Michael Garrett
Production Designer:	Derek Jarman
Cast:	Dorothy Tutin, Scott Anthony, Helen Mirren, Lindsay Kemp, Michael Gough, John Justin

MAHLER (UK, 1974, 115 MIN)

Production Company:	Goodtimes Enterprises
Director:	Ken Russell
Producer:	Roy Baird
Photography:	Dick Bush
Screenplay:	Ken Russell
Editor:	Michael Bradsell
Production Designer:	Ian Whittaker
Cast:	Robert Powell, Georgina Hale, Richard Morant, Lee Montague, Rosalie Crutchley, Benny Lee, David Collings

TOMMY (UK, 1975, 111 MIN)

Production Company:	Columbia
Director:	Ken Russell
Producer:	Robert Stigwood, Ken Russell
Photography:	Dick Bush, Ronnie Taylor
Screenplay:	Ken Russell (based on the musical drama by Pete Townshend, John Entwistle and Keith Moon)
Editor:	Stuart Baird
Production Designer:	Paul Dufficey
Music:	Pete Townshend, Roger Daltrey, John Entwistle and Keith Moon
Choreographer:	Gillian Gregory
Costume Designer:	Shirley Russell
Cast:	Ann-Margret, Oliver Reed, Roger Daltrey, Elton John, Eric Clapton, Jack Nicholson, Robert Powell, Paul Nicholas, Tina Turner, Barry Winch

LISZTOMANIA <small>(UK, 1975, 104 MIN)</small>

Production Company:	VPS, Goodtimes
Director:	Ken Russell
Producer:	Roy Baird, David Puttnam
Photography:	Peter Suschitzky
Screenplay:	Ken Russell
Production Designer:	Philip Harrison
Musical Director:	John Forsyth
Cast:	Roger Daltrey, Sara Kestelman, Paul Nicholas, Fiona Lewis, John Justin, Ringo Starr

VALENTINO <small>(UK, 1977, 127 MIN)</small>

Production Company:	Aperture
Director:	Ken Russell
Producer:	Chartoff-Winkler, Harry Benn
Photography:	Peter Suschitzky
Screenplay:	Ken Russell, Mardik Martin (from the book by Brad Steiger and Chaw Mank)
Music:	Ferde Grof, Stanley Black
Production Designer:	Philip Harrison
Cast:	Rudolf Nureyev, Leslie Caron, Michelle Phillips, Carol Kane, Felicity Kendall, Huntz Hall, David de Keyser, Alfred Marks, Anton Diffring, Jennie Linden, John Justin

ALTERED STATES <small>(UK, 1980, 102 MIN)</small>

Production Company:	Warner
Director:	Ken Russell
Producer:	Howard Gottfried, Daniel Melnick
Photography:	Jordan Cronenweth
Screenplay:	Sidney Aaron, Paddy Chayevsky (from the novel by Paddy Chayevsky)
Music:	John Corigliano
Production Designer:	Richard McDonald
Cast:	William Hurt, Blair Brown, Bob Balaban, Charles Haid

CRIMES OF PASSION <small>(UK, 1984, 104 MIN)</small>

Production Company:	New World
Director:	Ken Russell
Producer:	Barry Sandler
Photography:	Dick Bush
Production Designer:	Richard McDonald
Screenplay:	Barry Sandler
Music:	Rick Wakeman
Cast:	Kathleen Turner, Anthony Perkins, John Laughlin, Annie Potts

GOTHIC (UK, 1987, 90 MIN)

Production Company:	Virgin Visions
Director:	Ken Russell
Producer:	Penny Corke
Photography:	Mike Southon
Screenplay:	Stephen Volk
Editor:	Peter Davies
Music:	Thomas Dolby
Production Designer:	Christopher Hobbs
Cast:	Gabriel Byrne, Julian Sands, Natasha Richardson, Miriam Cyr, Timothy Spall

ARIA (UK, 1988, 98 MIN)

Production Company:	Warner
Co-Director:	Ken Russell (with Nicolas Roeg, Jean-Luc Godard, Derek Jarman, Robert Altman etc.)
Producer:	Don Boyd
Photography:	Gabriel Beristain
Screenplay:	Ken Russell
Music:	Giacomo Puccini
Editor:	Michael Bradsell
Production Designer:	Matthew Jacobs
Cast:	Linzi Drew, Andreas Wisniewski

THE LAIR OF THE WHITE WORM (UK, 1988, 93 MIN)

Production Company:	Vestron
Director:	Ken Russell
Producer:	Ken Russell
Photography:	Dick Bush
Screenplay:	Ken Russell (based on the novel by Bram Stoker)
Editor:	Peter Davies
Special Effects:	Geoff Portass
Music Director:	Stanislas Syrewicz
Cast:	Amanda Donohoe, Hugh Grant, Catherine Oxenberg, Peter Capaldi, Sammi Davis, Stratford Johns, Paul Brooke, Imogen Claire, Christopher Gable

SALOME'S LAST DANCE (UK, 1988, 90 MIN)

Production Company:	Jolly Russell Productions
Director:	Ken Russell
Producer:	Penny Corke
Photography:	Harvey Harrison
Screenplay:	Ken Russell (based on the play *Salome*, by Oscar Wilde)
Editor:	Timothy Gee
Production Designer:	Christopher Hobbs
Music Director:	Richard Cooke, Ray Beckett
Cast:	Glenda Jackson, Stratford Johns, Nicholas Grace, Douglas Hodge, Imogen Millais-Scott, Denis Lill, Ken Russell

THE RAINBOW (UK, 1989, 111 MIN)

Production Company:	Vestron
Director:	Ken Russell
Producer:	Ken Russell
Photography:	Billy Williams
Screenplay:	Ken Russell, Vivian Russell (based on the novel by DH Lawrence)
Editor:	Peter Davies
Production Designer:	Lucciana Arrighi
Music:	Carl Davis
Cast:	Sammi Davis, Paul McGann, Amanda Donohoe, Christopher Gable, David Hemmings, Glenda Jackson, Dudley Sutton, Jim Carter, Judith Paris, Ken Colley

WHORE (UK, 1991, 85 MIN)

Production Company:	Trimark
Director:	Ken Russell
Producer:	Dan Ireland, Ronaldo Vasconcellos
Photography:	Amir Mokri
Screenplay:	Ken Russell, Deborah Dalton (based on the play *Bondage*, by David Hines)
Editor:	Brian Tagg
Production Designer:	Richard Lewis
Music:	Michael Gibbs
Cast:	Theresa Russell, Benjamin Mouton, Antonio Fargas, Elizabeth Moorhead, Michael Crabtree

INDEX